We
need
to talk

We need to talk

The truth about sexual violence and my fight for justice

Emily Hunt

MARDLE

First published in 2023 by Mardle Books
15 Church Road
London, SW13 9HE
www.mardlebooks.com

Paperback ISBN 9781914451157
eBook ISBN 9781914451508

A CIP catalogue record for this book is available from the British Library.

Every reasonable effort has been made to trace copyright-holders of
material reproduced in this book, but if any have been inadvertently
overlooked the publishers would be glad to hear from them.

Printed in the UK

10 9 8 7 6 5 4 3 2 1

Cover credit: Shutterstock

For Mira,
who knows that if she wants to,
she can change the world.

A note on names

This story is mine.

Throughout, you will see that I have used the pseudonym "John" for my attacker. This is a conscious choice. I legally could name him, but I choose not to.

I've said his name in public exactly once – in court at his sentencing – and I don't plan to ever do so again. He's not worth it.

My story is not about him, it's what happened after I woke up in a bed next to him.

Fundamentally, this book isn't about naming and shaming, this book is about trying to change the way we talk about sexual violence in this country. To that end, in addition to the pseudonym for my attacker, I have made some choices on who to name and who not to name, mostly to give credit where it's due to the amazing people who have helped me along the way but also to not distract from the story or the bigger points by naming those who let me down.

There is something I need to tell you...

What I remember most – probably because it's what I remember first – was the feeling of the bedspread against my bare skin. It was insubstantial, and somehow both rough and soft at the same time. Curled up on my left side, cold, naked and shivering, its texture was confusing. It clearly wasn't mine.

I lay there and struggled to get my bearings; then, somewhere through the haze, I heard an unfamiliar voice in animated conversation on the phone. I couldn't really focus on what was being said, but I heard the man announce himself as "John" to the person at the other end of the line. The call ended, then there was the sound of flipping channels and the laughter of a man I didn't know.

I have no idea how much time passed in those moments or between them and the next. Slowly, as my eyes blinked open and I started to come around properly, I saw an unfamiliar room. I could see a couch and a coffee table from where I lay on the bed. Muted tones and high-end hotel furniture. I had no idea where I was. It quickly got worse. As I peered over my bare right shoulder, I had no idea who the man was whom I saw on the bed with me. He was fully clothed, languidly leaning against the headboard and enjoying whatever he had stumbled across on the television. *I had never seen him before in my life.*

He was clothed.

I was naked.

My memories of those pieces of time are a jumble, like something I'd seen somewhere a long time ago. But after the fog that lasted seemingly for hours as I drifted in and out, I remember the sensation of quite suddenly coming to. In the pit of my stomach a crawling feeling of panic started to grow. Nothing was making sense.

I peered down over the edge of the mattress and saw my clothes dropped in a pile by the side of the bed next to my handbag. Without even really thinking about it, I reached into my bag for my phone. I had maybe a dozen missed calls and texts from people who were wondering where I was. I had missed a dinner, I was very unusually not answering my phone and even my ex-husband was wondering where I was.

It was 10:22pm and the last thing I remembered was finishing up a long lunch with my dad at least five hours earlier. Maybe more.

I rolled over and faced the stranger in the bed. He was a white guy with short brown hair. His eyes were spaced perhaps a bit too far apart, much like his front teeth. He looked like just a regular guy, normal-looking, maybe a little ugly. He was extraordinarily ordinary, and instantly forgettable.

"Where am I?" I asked.

"At the Town Hall Hotel," he replied, and then he paused for a moment as the words hung in the air. "Do you know what my name is?"

I thought for a moment, inspecting this man's face for any sign of familiarity. There was none, and then the phone call I had overheard came back to me.

"John. Your name is John," I answered with near certainty.

Something was very wrong. It occurred to me suddenly that I'd probably been drugged. I felt the possibility of it completely in that moment. Many of us have had the classic big night out with parts forgotten, but I had never had a full five hours missing without so much as a foggy recollection of something embarrassing. Perhaps more telling, if I'd been drunk enough to miss five hours of my own life, I would still be drunk. Or I'd be throwing up. Or both. And I was neither. I started to grab my clothes and my phone from the floor.

Numb and shaking, I went to hide in the bathroom.

It's only now, through what I've been told, that I know any of what happened to me in those previous five hours.

What happened to me afterwards still defies logic and belief.

What is clear, though, is that I was in control of none of it.

Chapter One

Ten and a half hours earlier, just before midday on a bright Sunday afternoon in East London, I walked into my favourite local restaurant to meet my dad for lunch. Light streamed in the windows, carrying spring inside. I was wearing a much-loved dress: black and quilted with three-quarter length sleeves and a skirt that hit above the knee. I was wearing my glasses, hadn't put on any make-up and was fidgeting with the long bronze chain-link necklace I loved to wear. It might have been bright out, but it was still chilly enough that I was wearing tights along with my trainers.

My dad and I ordered coffee and waited for the day's lunch menu to be written up on the blackboard on the far wall. From our table in the corner, I watched the restaurant filling up around me. At midday, we drank wine while we considered what to have for lunch.

I was at this pivotal moment in my life. It was as though everything was starting over. My divorce had just been finalised, I was interviewing for an amazing job the next day – and had a date planned that evening with the sort of man my father desperately wanted me to marry: a lawyer, at a bank. Though I was born in New York, I've lived in London longer than I've lived anywhere else in my life. Similarly, though born in the States, my dad had lived in Ireland for the better part of 40 years. Whenever he came to visit, we found ourselves in the same restaurant, settling in for a long meal and an even longer conversation.

"I just want you to find someone who will take care of you so you can have more babies," my father said, apparently unaware of how ridiculous it sounded.

While I did very much want to meet the right man and have more kids, I wasn't in a rush. I'd already been married to the wrong one, and we'd had a wonderful baby girl together five years earlier. I knew what it was like to do that with the wrong person. I didn't want to repeat that mistake just for the sake of financial security or more children. I'd always been the breadwinner in our house, but my dad never quite understood that I loved my career and was happy working in a big job: that what I really wanted, then, was to get an even bigger job; I had high ambitions for myself.

Food arrived, more wine came, too, and after the meal was done, we each ordered a grappa. My dad was going to the airport for his flight to Dublin just after lunch. We were both choosing to ignore the fact that the weekend had been a bit of a long "last hurrah". We both knew that the next day, he'd be finding out for sure if he had cancer and what his options were going to be. He'd already decided that if it was going to be a long and difficult battle, he wasn't going to do it. His brother had been losing to the same kind of cancer for a decade and he didn't want to do the same thing. We'd spent the weekend walking around London, eating amazing food and even giving him a bit of a makeover. I was feeling very "next day, rest of my life", with everything about to take off in the right direction, all the time conscious that the next few days could take my father down a very different road.

I ordered another grappa and my dad ordered a coffee. It was getting late and he was going to need to get his suitcase from my house before getting in a taxi.

He had a sip of my grappa – and then that's when things started to get very strange. Our conversation tilted. My dad started saying really odd things and I think I sort of remember him getting up to leave the restaurant. I definitely remember ordering him a taxi – but then there is nothing. It is completely blank.

One moment I was in a local favourite restaurant; the next, more than five hours later, I woke up naked in bed next to a stranger.

I called a friend from the hotel bathroom. I was scared and confused and not making much sense. I didn't sound drunk but I was incoherent. The friend thought I sounded like I was on drugs, something he knew I'd never done in my life. When I told him that the man I had woken up next to was still in the hotel room, he decided to call the police. After we hung up – and knowing that help was on the way – I stayed in the bathroom, redressing step by step, underwear on one leg at a time, reaching behind my back to clasp my bra, before pulling my dress

on over my head and putting on my shoes. I started
to feel that something that should be impossible had
happened, something completely out of my control.
I left the tights in my handbag because, in all hones-
ty, I wanted out of that hotel. Fast. I couldn't find
my necklace.

When I came back into the room, John tried to
smooth the situation over. It was clear that I was
visibly shaken, so first he told me that nothing
had happened. That we hadn't had sex. He said I
shouldn't leave, that I should stay longer with him.
He was getting increasingly persistent and I was
getting more and more scared.

Then he said he'd like to see me again.

"That would be great," I said, grabbing a piece of
paper. "What's your number? And your surname?"
I asked sweetly, smiling through gritted teeth.

I knew two things. First, the police were on their
way and I just had to stay safe for a few more minutes.
Second, that it would probably be really helpful for the
police if I could name my attacker. Maybe he could
read my thoughts from the expression on my face,
because when he carefully spelled out his surname he

swapped some of the letters, and when he gave me his number it was missing a digit. I told him I'd call him soon, and then headed for the door, trying not to show any panic.

As I shut the door behind me, my phone rang from a blocked number. The police were calling to tell me that they were downstairs. I gave them the hotel room number – something I could only do because I was standing in front of the door – and went running down the stairs into the shining lobby of the hotel.

I don't remember anything about the police officer at the bottom of the stairs who caught me on my way down. They held me for a moment. I must have been shaking. Crying. But I mostly remember the tiles on the floor of the lobby, the lights from above, the roughness of what must have been a zipper on the officer's jacket. I pointed up the stairs, repeated the hotel room number and was led out of the building.

The next thing I remember was collapsing onto the grass outside, the world tunnelling in front of me, and hearing the ragged sound of my own breath as I began to panic.

I had never had a full-blown hyperventilating panic attack before. The feeling of being unable to get air in, dragging air through my mouth as fast as it would come but having my body in full collapse below me. I couldn't move, I couldn't breathe; it felt unending, until slowly my breath started to come back to me. As the panic attack subsided, I heard the police phoning for an ambulance. They picked me up off the ground and put me into the back of a waiting police car. Though terrified of what had just happened, I could see from inside the car swarms of police going in and out of the hotel lobby. In that instant I felt safe. I saw the police and thought that everything was going to be okay. They were there and everything would be taken care of. I would be safe.

I am not a witness to my own rape.[1] The facts that I know now have taken days, months and years to put together since that bright May day. They are drawn from the summary of John's statement to the police, witness accounts, descriptions of what was on CCTV, lab reports and many conversations with

---

1   My position continues to be that John deserved to defend himself in court against this allegation, and it was unfair of the Crown Prosecution Service not to give him this opportunity. I think that the evidence – which is not in dispute – speaks for itself, but a jury should decide.

lawyers and journalists, as well as meetings with the Metropolitan Police and Crown Prosecution Service. The details of what happened in the hours before I woke up in bed next to John are only what I've been told.

After my dad left the restaurant,[2] I apparently stayed there for a while longer. The staff said I didn't seem drunk or too worse for wear. But my ex-husband, James,[3] had been surprised that my dad had seemed so out of it when he came to collect his suitcase. He said he'd never seen my dad so drunk, and he was surprised, as we hadn't been gone that long and my father could very much hold his liquor.

James and I had been divorced for three months, but it was a hugely amicable divorce at the start – so much so that he was still living in the house with me and our five-year-old daughter. When he saw the state my father was in he started worrying about me. And

---

2   In my original statement given to police a few days later, I put the time that my dad left at between 5 and 6pm. I hadn't yet spoken with my dad and I was later able to determine that as my dad made it onto his flight to Dublin, we must have parted ways between 4 and 5, but definitely before 5pm.

3   My ex-husband requested a pseudonym be used. I let our daughter pick a name for him, and she decided that he should be called "James".

Chapter One

I wasn't answering my phone. He rang the restaurant and asked them to tell me to answer my phone. When he finally got through to me, I apparently told him that I was talking with a guy and I'd be home later. I don't remember the conversation at all.

Probably an hour after that conversation I walked into Poison, a small bar with a neon sign out front that flicked from "Poison" to "Cleanse" depending on whether it was open or not. I'd never been inside this bar, but I had seen it from the outside. They were having a psychedelic movie event, and the space must have been glowing from the lights of the film.

"Are you on drugs?" John asked pretty immediately once we started speaking. I was holding a glass with clear liquid in it. He was having a hard time following what I was saying. I was repeating myself and talking about a restaurant.

He told the police later that I seemed like I might be a bit crazy. For some reason John was on his own that Sunday afternoon in this small bar on the far side of town from where he lived. He wasn't drinking and had no drugs in his system. He had condoms and drugs in his rucksack, however, that he later told the police were LSD and Viagra.

We walked into the Town Hall Hotel less than an hour after I had arrived in Poison. CCTV along the way shows me to be very intoxicated,[4] with my arms flopped down at my side, my gait very unsteady and leaning on John at various points along the way to the hotel.

As John and I stood at the check-in desk, the hotel receptionist thought we were a couple. I was leaning on John to steady myself. We held hands. The receptionist said later that while I seemed very tired, she didn't think anything was amiss. We could have been anyone. John mentioned to her that I'd had a bit too much to drink and just needed to rest for a while. As we headed up to the room, I became even less steady on my feet. In fact, as John opened the door to our hotel room, the CCTV recorded me falling backwards, completely unable to remain standing on my own. I happened to land on a bench; if it hadn't been there, I would have landed on the floor. John walked into the hotel room, and I followed behind. The door shut behind us.

---

4   According to a police officer who re-reviewed the CCTV in 2021, there is no mistaking that I am extremely intoxicated in the video.

As we undressed, John took his condoms out of his rucksack. He asked if he needed them and I made a comment about being the sort of person who gets pregnant. Apparently, that was enough to convince him to use them. However, while we were having sex, he was having difficulty and couldn't keep an erection. He told the police that I passed out immediately after he stopped having sex with me.[5, 6] He then got dressed and went down to reception

5   In my original police statement, I said that I thought I must have been unconscious when John had sex with me because I had no knowledge or memory of it and didn't recognise him at all when I woke up. But over the years, after I learned more about the impact of date-rape drugs like GHB and was told the details from John's statement to the police, I assumed that I was conscious but deeply intoxicated. However, in August 2021, John tweeted what appears to be a confession of having sex with me while I was unconscious: "I was basically impotent, and I had sex with her for a few seconds. She woke up and I told her 'nothing' had happened. I was embarrassed and I wanted to forget about the experience. For this, I have been called a rapist." Having sex with someone who then wakes up is having sex with someone who is not conscious, and therefore unable to give consent. That is rape and that is illegal. Unfortunately, as in the case of Bonny Turner, the Crown Prosecution Service doesn't seem to accept written confessions as sufficient evidence of rape to take a case forward.

6   For more information on Bonny Turner's story: https://www.theguardian.com/society/2020/jul/30/survivor-talks-of-gas-lighting-of-victims-ahead-of-judicial-review

to deal with an issue with his credit card, before coming back up and turning on the hotel room's television. And then, after a while, I woke up.

While I was collapsing outside the hotel, the police went to the room and asked John to come out into the hallway. The CCTV footage shows him fairly relaxed and joking around a bit with the police. It then shows him trying to ditch his drugs there in the corridor as they take him away to the police station to be interviewed under caution. There were used condoms in the room. They never found my necklace.

The police had been called immediately and it seemed like it should have been a straightforward case. Whether I was drunk or drugged, I was obviously impaired as John had asked me if I was on drugs and had told the police he thought I was possibly mentally ill. I couldn't even reliably stand up on my own, and there is CCTV footage of me falling over right before going into the hotel room with him. He not only admitted to the sex, but there were also used condoms at the scene. But, as happens to the majority of rape victims, the system failed me: the police investigation was doomed from the start.

Chapter One

I was taken to the local hospital in an ambulance. I was hypoglycemic, having trouble breathing and complaining of chest pains. I was left in a curtained-off cubicle in A&E while numerous, nameless nurses, doctors and uniformed police officers came and went, while I had no sense of what was happening. I was shaking under a hospital blanket and blinded by the fluorescent light. Everything hurt. After a while, a young female cop, dwarfed by her uniform, came in and started asking questions. She'd been in and out with the rest, but it appeared that she'd been charged with taking care of me. She asked a few questions and disappeared again.

She returned well after midnight with a white box containing the early evidence collection kit. She took out the instructions, carefully unfolding them and smoothing them out. She started at the top, reading through. It seemed to me this was perhaps her first time and she wanted to get it right. There weren't the swabs you see on TV; in fact, there was nothing more intimate than peeing in a cup. I dutifully went off to the bathroom to provide the sample. By now it was the early hours of the morning.

What neither I, nor likely even the young police officer, realised, was that it was already far too late. Most date-rape drugs, like GHB, metabolise out of the victim's system within six to twelve hours,[7] which means that when the police first arrived at the scene sometime after 10:30pm, the window was already closing, as I'd likely been drugged around six hours earlier. So it is possible that even if I had given a sample when I first arrived at the hospital, it would have been too late. I don't remember exactly what was said when we arrived, but I know that no one explained the time crunch; no one explained that the evidence was disappearing as each second passed; no one handed me a glass of water and told me it was important to be able to pee right then and there.

When I came back with the filled sample cup, the policewoman explained – reading from the instruction sheet – that they would take another sample an hour later to compare with the first.

"That way we can see how quickly things are metabolising," she said. "Also, if you could have

---

7 Haller C., Thai D., Jacob P,. and Dyer J.E. (2006), "GHB Urine Concentrations After Single-Dose Administration in Humans: (National Institutes of Health)

someone bring you some clothes, that would be great. We need what you're wearing for evidence."

I asked about a blood test, as I thought that would be more accurate, but she said that wasn't part of the evidence collection. With her job done, she left the cubicle.

It was around two o'clock in the morning when I rang a few friends to see if anyone could bring me some clothes. It was a horrifying task. I was afraid that someone would answer and I would have to explain why I was calling: to borrow some clothes. Worse, if they did answer, I would then likely have to tell them that I thought I'd probably been raped. Though I rang five different people, no one answered. I told the police that no one was available to bring me clothes. Years later, I found out that they wrote down in their notebooks that I'd refused to give them clothes as evidence and was being difficult. Because I had no clothes to change into and no friends able to answer the phone at 2am, they began to doubt I was a rape victim.

I had been asking when they would be taking me for an examination to make sure that I was okay and wasn't injured. I assumed they wanted to take more evidence, or that they could find me something to wear so they could take my clothes. The uniformed officers said they wouldn't be taking me for a forensic examination – even though they had told the hospital that they would be – and that someone would be in touch the next day with information on how to get to the Haven, the local specialist rape centre run in partnership between the NHS and the Metropolitan Police. In the end, they said I couldn't give my consent for a forensic medical examination in my condition – seven hours after John had sex with me, the police said I still seemed too intoxicated.

It was nearly three o'clock in the morning as we walked down the little road to my house. I was shattered, emotionally and physically. I felt as though I'd run a marathon. The police officer had finally managed to get hold of someone from the Sapphire Unit, London's sexual offences unit. They'd apparently been promising to turn up on the scene for hours but hadn't been able to. She handed me the phone, and on the other end was a woman whose name I didn't catch.

Chapter One

"Right, I can be there in about an hour and a half to take your statement," she said. Stunned, I started to cry. I'd been with the police since not long after 10:30pm. It was five hours later and this woman wanted me to wait another 90 minutes. It would have been 4:30 or 5 in the morning after a very long and traumatic day. I literally couldn't do it. We agreed I'd speak with them the next day about giving a statement.

I let the police who had taken me home into the house and went upstairs into the bathroom to do the second urine sample and to change out of my clothes into pyjamas. I walked into my bedroom as though wading through molasses, tired and slow.

Standing next to my bed, a police officer opened an evidence bag and told me to put my dress in it. Robotically, one by one, each article of clothing went into a separate bag which was then sealed in front of me. As they finished up, they told me not to shower. They said someone would be in touch the next day. Then they left.

In the suddenly quiet house, with my daughter asleep in her room and my ex-husband asleep downstairs, I fell over into my bed, the world quickly receding as exhaustion took hold. I was asleep in moments.

Sometime after dawn, I woke up to my daughter kissing my nose. She had just turned five the week before and morning was our time together. We always spent at least half an hour in bed together first thing in the morning, having breakfast, hanging out and talking about our day.

I thought that I would be too destroyed that morning to deal with being a mother, but I broke out in a huge smile at the silliness of the beautiful face squished up against mine. I pulled her into my bed and gave her the sort of hug that only mums can really give. She wriggled away and giggled and settled down next to me to start telling me about the goings on in her reception class. Luckily, that morning, for whatever reason, she didn't ask about my day.

What I didn't know is that by the time I was spending that precious time with my daughter, I'd already done everything wrong as a victim.

I hadn't rung the police, my friend had, so I was attention-seeking. I'd hyperventilated and needed an ambulance, so was overreacting and carrying on. At the hospital, I'd refused to give my clothes as evidence, and so was being difficult and untrustworthy. Finally, I'd refused to give my statement to the police at 4:30 in the morning. Perhaps that was the final straw? I'll never know what exactly it was about me or what specific moment it was that made the police decide my case wasn't worth pursuing, but the decision had already been made by those small hours of the morning, only twelve hours after I'd woken up in bed next to a stranger. I was not a worthy victim. Every perceived "mistake" I made that night meant that my case didn't have a chance.

Much like I wasn't a direct witness to what happened in the hours before waking up in the hotel bed next to John, I also wasn't a witness to or even particularly involved in the police investigation in the months that followed. From feeling like John had taken control of my body, I was then made to feel even more powerless by the police.

My knowledge of the initial investigation comes from many of the same sources that helped me piece together the time between my dad leaving the restaurant and me waking up five hours later. But it's full of holes: there are so many things I still don't know and many things I will likely never get to the bottom of.

From the beginning, my case was never prioritised. I do actually understand why the case of a woman who wakes up in a nice hotel with no memory of what happened might be treated as a lower priority than the truly heinous things seen on a daily basis by the sex offences unit of a major metropolitan police department. But as I had also been perceived as an unworthy victim, my case dropped even lower. Unfortunately, the police's lack of urgency meant that by the time they actually went looking for evidence, a lot of it wasn't there.

It took a few weeks for the police to take statements from staff at the restaurant where I'd had lunch with my father. They spoke to hotel staff even later than that, and never took statements from people in the bar where John claims we met. They never investigated the guy I told my ex-husband I was speaking with in the restaurant, or tried to establish if any patrons at the bar saw me talking to John. As far as I am aware, they didn't look for CCTV evidence showing how I got from the restaurant to the bar. They didn't request a hair test from me, despite this being a useful back-up when a urine sample is too late to show anything. They didn't test my clothes. Perhaps most amazing of all, they didn't test the drugs that John had with him. To be clear: they made no effort to follow up on the fact that this man – who had been accused of drugging someone – was found in possession of drugs.

The biggest problem was one that I wouldn't fully find out about for nearly a year, and it's probably what ultimately destroyed any hope I had of my attacker being charged in 2015.

When the police were filling in the paperwork for the toxicology lab to accompany my urine sample, they wrote that I was probably drugged around 7:00pm. My last memory is two and a half to three hours earlier than that. As my father was clearly also drugged and then left for the airport, I can't have been drugged even as late as 5:00pm. Based on this inaccurate timeline, the toxicology lab concluded that I'd definitely not been drugged.

That wouldn't have been a problem in itself – even if I had "just" been drunk, so drunk to the point of completely losing five hours of time and being unable to stand reliably on my own, it still would have shown any reasonable person that I couldn't possibly have given consent for sex. But the toxicology lab also proved that I couldn't have been that drunk. My blood alcohol content was only twice the legal limit for driving, nowhere near drunk enough for a straightforward consent case on the basis of the lab result alone. The fact that I *appeared* drunk – so drunk, in fact, that the police believed I was still too intoxicated hours after the sex to give consent for a medical exam – but did not have enough alcohol in my body to explain my condition, along with the fact that I was hypoglycemic in the ambulance, *should* have pointed to a drugging. Instead, it was counted as just another ding against my case.

Late in July, two and a half months after the incident, a police officer rang me to tell me that the police were passing my case to the Crown Prosecution Service to ask for a decision on whether or not to charge my attacker. At this point she mentioned that the toxicology had come back showing no drugs in my system. She did not, however, mention that my blood alcohol content had come back so low. Not knowing that detail, however, I breathed a sigh of relief. I thought that the outcome would be obvious: that in a year or so, there would be a trial. That it would be up to a jury and that although it would be hard for me, there was a real chance that my attacker would go to prison. I also thought that if I hadn't been drugged, then at least I wouldn't have to prove who had drugged me, and when and where it had happened. It was cleaner, more straightforward, even if it meant that I'd gotten myself so drunk I'd been unable to give my consent for sex. I assumed that the prosecutors were deeply interested in prosecuting sex offenders and that I would be safe in their hands. It never occurred to me that the CPS could choose not to prosecute once the police sent them the case.

So I was both surprised and heartbroken in September 2015, six months after the event, when I was told that my case was not going forward due to insufficient evidence.

Two weeks later, a follow-up letter arrived in response to my request that they review the decision to not prosecute John. It included much more detail about the evidence and essentially said that I was drunk – but not too drunk – and that John had no reasonable way of knowing I couldn't or wouldn't consent to sex with him. It was my first look at a few breadcrumbs of the facts of the case, and the first time any pieces were dropped into my five-hour blackout.

I decided that the CPS must be right. That it must have been my fault. So I didn't appeal again.

And that, I thought, was that.

In May 2016, just over a year since I'd woken up next to John, I was sitting in a brightly lit conference room at work, waiting for Detective Inspector Roger Leigh[8] and a female colleague of his, Ellen Green, to arrive.

In the week following the incident, I had filed a complaint against the police for their behaviour towards me and for their failure to properly gather evidence. I'd been told that this meeting was to give me an update on that original complaint.

DI Leigh was in charge of investigating my complaint, even though he worked with the same team that I'd made the complaint about. He had emailed me the week before, asking for the meeting.

_____

8   Names have been changed.

Chapter One

He told me that the meeting was to update me on the issues I had raised.

It wasn't.

When they arrived in the conference room, I was feeling in charge of the situation for once. I had had a deeply difficult year. But 10 months after the assault, I was finally diagnosed with PTSD – and the fog had started to lift.

The police officers sat across the smooth white table from me and began to explain that there were two things about that night I was unaware of.

The first was that John had taken a video of me naked and unconscious on the hotel bed. On the night of his arrest, he'd told the police that he took the video to masturbate to later, and that he knew he didn't have my permission to take it. For a minute and two seconds, the video shows my back, my buttocks, then his face, and then returns to my body.

As they told me about the video, I could feel the blood draining from my face. As DI Leigh finished, I apologised, said I needed a moment and fled the room. I made it as far as the conference room across the hall, where I held on to the edge of a chair and tried to hold back tears. I was afraid I was going to throw up. I definitely no longer felt in control.

After composing myself, I went back into the room and started asking questions.

"Did he upload the video anywhere?" I asked.

"I don't know what you mean," DI Leigh said.

"I mean, before the police confiscated his phone, did he have a chance to upload that video to the Cloud? Does he still have it? Did he send it to anyone?" I asked, getting increasingly worried, with panic rising in my voice.

"Oh, I don't know," DI Leigh said, "but I can ask the tech guys to check the data download to see if they can tell."

I sat silently, staring in disbelief. How could they have not thought to check whether or not my attacker had managed to keep a copy of this video? How could they have not thought to tell me all of this until now? But more importantly, I wondered, how on earth could they not be thinking of this as a crime, a crime for which John should be held to account? I was being told this information very much as an afterthought.

Chapter One

My mind was reeling as the police officer went on to tell me the second thing I hadn't been told about at the time. In addition to taking the video, John had apparently masturbated next to me[9] as I slept, with his leg over my leg and while touching my hand. He then ejaculated onto my thigh.[10] He told the police all of this in his original statement when he'd been arrested a year earlier. But no one had told me.

I was at a loss to understand why they had this incriminating statement from my attacker, but never prosecuted him for taking the video and for assaulting me, even if rape was too difficult to prove given the failures of the police investigation.

The end of the meeting was a blur. I went back to work. I went through the motions of everything I was supposed to do. But I couldn't shake the feeling something was really wrong with what the police had told me: they'd waited so long to tell me and they didn't seem to think there should be any further consequences as a result of this information. I just

---

9 It is unclear from the police file if he was just touching my hand while he did this or using my hand to masturbate.
10 This would normally be considered sexual assault.

couldn't understand why they'd bothered to tell me now, but I also couldn't understand why they hadn't told me any of this in the first place.

Later that week, I sat down to figure out what I should do. I went back to the October 2015 letter from the CPS which confirmed that following their review, they'd decided they'd still not be prosecuting John. That letter had provided that first glimpse into what had happened, but never mentioned amongst the list of weaknesses in my evidence that John had taken a video of me naked without my consent, nor that he had masturbated on to me while I was asleep.

I had also learned a few more things since that letter. As small pieces of the jigsaw puzzle of that night started to fall into place, it was becoming clear that I'd been unbelievably naïve in trusting the police and the CPS to properly investigate a sex offence case. And it was starting to feel that there was perhaps another way.

I emailed the Crown Prosecution Service asking them to explain why, even if the rape case had gone nowhere, they hadn't prosecuted my attacker on the basis of the video or the fact he'd masturbated onto me.

Chapter One

It took them five months to meet with me, only to claim it was not illegal to video someone naked without their consent. They then directly contradicted what the police had told me, saying my attacker hadn't masturbated onto me, but onto the bed instead.

Both would turn out not to be true.

By the end of the meeting I was hurt, confused and totally bewildered. It made no sense to me that they still wouldn't do anything to help me, that John would never be charged and there would never be any measure of justice.

But then, after the meeting, a solicitor acquaintance who had come along to represent me took me into a pub across the street from the CPS's office, ordered me a very large glass of white wine and started to explain my options. Because, much to my surprise, I did have some.

Chapter Two

Imagine you are sitting in a fairly full train carriage anywhere in England. Imagine all of the people around you, on their way to work or just heading off on a day out. Now think about the women who probably account for about half the passengers on the train. They would be every sort of age, from every sort of background, all of them the same sort of women seen every day, in every train carriage. Let's say there are 40 of these women in the carriage around you. In all probability, around eight of them have been sexually assaulted.

You can engage in the same sort of thought experiment on the people you see every day, around the office or at school. People you see on the street or in shops. Your friends. Even your family. Changing the audience doesn't matter. Regardless of who the women are that you are imagining, around a fifth have been sexually assaulted or been the victim of an attempted sexual assault in the course of their lives.

That's seven million women in this country.

Just imagine these figures for a moment. It's the whole of the population of London. It is estimated that 85,000 women and 12,000 men are raped each year in England and Wales[11] – and this is assumed to be a very conservative estimate. In 2021, the government put the total at around 128,000 rape victims a year.[12]

Before this happened to me, I had no idea how a rape investigation worked. In fact, I had no idea how the criminal justice system really worked at all. I had no idea of how inefficient or under-resourced it is. More importantly, I had no idea how prevalent sexual violence is or how much of an impact it has. Perhaps worst of all, I had no idea how many people

---

11   https://rapecrisis.org.uk/get-informed/about-sexual-violence/statistics-sexual-violence/

12   https://assets.publishing.service.gov.uk/government/uploads/system/uploads/attachment_data/file/1001417/end-to-end-rape-review-report-with-correction-slip.pdf

I knew had been raped. Even though I speak publicly about rape – and even though countless strangers have now got in touch with me to tell me their stories – I still have no idea how many women and men I know, personally or professionally, who have been raped. It's just not something that we talk about.

There is a very human reaction to the idea of rape: to assume that it occurs to other people, that it happens infrequently, that rapists are loners, losers and obvious monsters. That we don't know people who have been affected. That it has nothing to do with us and our lives. That we're safe from such things. The image of rape that we carry with us is of a woman walking home on a darkened street and being dragged into the bushes by a stranger. Even then, it's almost natural instinct to start to put the blame on the victim:

What was she wearing?

Had she been drinking?

Why was she walking alone at night?

What had she done to entice this man?

Hadn't her father taught her how to protect herself?

Even now I have to stop myself sometimes from straying into this way of thinking because it feels so normal and natural. We have all been conditioned.

Chapter Two

Just because no one has ever told you they've been raped, that doesn't mean that you don't know any victims. You do. You know plenty of them.

Sexual violence is an undeniable fact of life for 20% of women in our country. Not only is rape prevalent, but it's also a crime that is very difficult for victims to talk about. Their silence, even with close friends and family, often means it feels impossible to understand or is simply irrelevant to our everyday lives.

In January 2018, I sat in a pub across the street from Parliament with Emily Jacob and Winnie M. Li, two women I didn't really know. The three of us had just been at an event at the House of Lords, and it was the first time I'd ever been in a room with other rape victims who were speaking about their experiences. It had been a revelation, both from the perspective of not feeling alone in what I'd experienced, but also adding a full measure of horror with the knowledge that so many other people had been through what I'd been through. Afterwards, we sat around a sticky wooden pub table and took turns buying rounds and crisps, talking about our experiences. The three of us and our experiences couldn't have been more different.

We were within about five years of each other in age, all well-educated and single, but that's where the similarities end.

Winnie had been on a trip to Northern Ireland, out hiking on her own near Belfast. She'd travelled the world on her own and had a full and vibrant career in film production. She'd been in Belfast for work but enjoying the hills for fun. She was wearing her favourite hiking shirt when a young man followed her on the trail and then assaulted her violently after pulling her into the undergrowth. She fled and was able to get help immediately. A horrified press covered her story in detail and the police worked to identify her assailant. Her friends and family rallied to her side. Her rapist was caught, charged and pleaded guilty just before the trial was due to start.

Emily Jacob had recently exited a bad marriage and was getting back into dating. She'd had a few big roles at work and was balancing a corporate career with the desire to do something more. She'd met a man online and was excited about the date – but her memory of the evening is fuzzy and she woke up in her bed knowing that something was wrong. She realised later that she must have been drugged. It took her a month to get up the courage to report her assault to the police and, by then, she wasn't even sure what she'd been wearing. It was too late for a standard toxicology screening. The police discounted her case but during the investigation found naked photos of her on her assailant's phone. They said it proved that she'd consented to the sex, even though she'd consented neither to the photos nor the sex. In fact, the photos should have shown that her attacker was the sort of person to take trophies. The CPS declined to charge him for lack of evidence. Emily J felt very much unsupported and disbelieved by the police.

As we exchanged our stories, the details of our experiences came flooding out. "The police gave me back my dress, in an unopened evidence bag," I said. "It's shoved in the back of my closet. I don't know what to do with it, but I keep thinking maybe someday it will be useful." After a pause, I added, "It was my favourite dress."

"When I got my clothes back, I started wearing them again. I pretty much wore the shirt until it fell apart. It was my favourite one," replied Winnie.

Emily J shook her head. "They didn't take my clothes, because I wasn't totally sure what I was wearing. But they did take my sheets. I don't think they did anything with them though. I threw them out when I got them back."

Winnie is the only person I know who has told me about their rape and received justice. But her rape is one of the very small number of stranger rapes in the UK: only about 1 in 10 fall into this category.[13] The mental image most of us have of rape applies far too often, but whilst it is a horrifying truth that a woman is raped by a stranger every hour, it is even more shocking to realise that women are attacked by people they know roughly every seven minutes.

Inevitably, when talking about rape, it becomes important to define it. But the way that each of our stories is so different, and is viewed so differently, begins to show just how tricky it is to define rape.

Rape of course has a legal definition, but it also has societal and personal ideas and definitions attached to it. For some people, it's easy: rape is sex without clear, positive, affirmative consent. But for others, it isn't that simple at all. We imagine rape like my earlier example, what television and

---

13   https://rapecrisis.org.uk/get-informed/about-sexual-violence/
statistics-sexual-violence/

movies show us: a stranger in the shadows, stalking a woman down the street before dragging her into the bushes and assaulting her. That kind of rape is easier to understand.

The legal definition of rape is very narrow: it is defined in England and Wales as "the intentional penetration of another person's vagina, anus, or mouth with the perpetrator's penis without consent or reasonable belief of consent".[14]

By this definition, there is little personal account-ability or responsibility around giving or receiving consent because it hinges on "reasonable belief"; worse, it is entirely subjective. In Winnie's case, it's easy to see: the stranger knew that he didn't have consent to follow her on that trail and rape her in the woods.

In my case, it comes down to: does John saying that he thought I might be on drugs or a bit mad, and my falling over, amount to him reasonably knowing that I could not have given consent for sex, or, rather, that a reasonable person would know that I couldn't have given consent? The CPS decid-ed that in my case, he or any reasonable person could have genuinely thought that while I was so

---

14   Sexual Offences Act of 2003.

obviously intoxicated to the point of not being able to reliably stand on my own, and not even necessarily knowing who I was with, as long as I said that I was up for sex, he had my consent.

To me, on the other hand, it seems that a reasonable person would look at the CCTV footage, see me unable to reliably stand on my own, and conclude that I couldn't possibly have given consent. This reasonable assumption is only made stronger by the fact that the police even refused to take me for a forensic medical examination because, in their opinion, I was too intoxicated to give consent to it more than seven hours after the sex occurred.

But the reality is that in the UK, one person in 10 believes that having sex with someone who is extremely drunk or even someone who is *asleep* isn't necessarily rape.[15]

In Emily J's case, she didn't consent to being drugged and definitely didn't consent to being raped, but her attacker told the police that she had wanted to have sex with him and that it had been consensual.

---

15   https://www.endviolenceagainstwomen.org.uk/wp-content/uploads/1-Attitudes-to-sexual-consent-Research-findings-FINAL.pdf

Her case was entirely he-said-she-said because the assault happened in her home and there was a lack of evidence. Of these three examples, Emily J's is most typical of the rapes that happen throughout the UK – except perhaps that unlike 85% of rape victims, she reported her rape to the police.[16]

As we've already learned, around 90% of rapes are committed by someone the victim knows.[17] And that makes things confusing. It is understandable that some people find it more difficult to accept that what happened to my friend Emily J, is as straightforward a case of rape as what happened to my friend Winnie, or even what happened to me. But it's still rape, even if it's harder to understand.

At the start of this chapter, as you sat and thought about the random women in a train carriage, I reminded you that anyone could be on that train. Part of the point of that thought exercise is that there is no particular type of rape victim. Unfortunately,

---

16   https://webarchive.nationalarchives.gov.uk/ukgwa/ 20160106113426/http://www.ons.gov.uk/ons/rel/crime-stats/ an-overview-of-sexual-offending-in-england---wales/decem- ber-2012/index.html

17   https://rapecrisis.org.uk/get-informed/about-sexual-violence/ statistics-sexual-violence/

the demographics of rape victims aren't particularly tracked in the UK. The Crime Survey for England and Wales shows only that women are much more likely to be sexually assaulted than men, and that young people are more likely to be assaulted than older people.[18] In the US, 90% of rape victims are female.[19] The vast majority of rape victims are under 35: 12% of victims are between 12 and 17 and 58% are between 18 and 34.[20] 28% of rape victims are 35–64 years old.[21] When it happened to me – and when it happened to Winnie and when it happened to Emily – we were all in that 18–64 category.

Beyond that, however, there aren't particularly solid statistics on rape victims, or the type of women who are more likely to be assaulted. There is a very simple reason for this: recent research conducted on over 7,000 previously unprocessed, untested sexual assault kits in the United States[22]

---

18   https://www.ons.gov.uk/peoplepopulationandcommunity/crimeandjustice/articles/sexualoffendingvictimisationandtheepaththroughthecriminaljusticesystem/2018-12-13

19   https://www.rainn.org/statistics/victims-sexual-violence
20   *ibid.*
21   *ibid.*
22   https://psycnet.apa.org/record/2019-28866-001

has shown not just the prevalence of serial offenders, but that even serial rapists do not assault any one type of woman. This data, from forensic evidence gathered from rape victims but warehoused for years instead of being processed, gives us a new and very different perspective on rape victims and their attackers. It's not that I was my rapist's type, or that Winnie's rapist had a preference for Asian women or that Emily J's rapist liked to assault women on a first date. We, as the victims, had very little to do with it.

Not only will a serial rapist rape a white woman in one instance and a black woman in another, a young blonde one time and an older grey-haired woman another – they won't necessarily stick to raping only strangers or only people they know. The conceit of countless television shows' portrayals of police hunting down the monster who preys on ponytailed, late 20s brunettes he has never met before, just doesn't bear out the facts.

Indeed, it was through this surprising discovery that investigators analysing a backlog of previously unprocessed and untested DNA evidence from rape cases in Cleveland, Ohio, found that some of their stranger-rape cases could actually be solved by evidence from acquaintance-rape cases.[23] They had always previously assumed that if a rapist attacked strangers, he wouldn't go after people he knew, and vice versa. That turned out to be an entirely false assumption. If rapists don't have a type of woman that they rape, we simply cannot pretend that there is a type or demographic of rape victim – aside from by and large being female and under the age of 65. This is a crime that can, and does, affect anyone in that rather large demographic and beyond.

Given that most rapes are committed by someone the victim knows, it isn't too surprising that rape often happens at home.[24] For some people, understanding the line of what is and isn't acceptable gets confused when the victim and the rapist know each other.

As an example, in a nationally representative survey from 2016, YouGov[25] found that a third of

23   https://www.theatlantic.com/magazine/archive/2019/08/an-epidemic-of-disbelief/592807/

24   https://web.archive.org/web/20200921182423/https://www.cps.gov.uk/legal-guidance/rape-and-sexual-offences-chapter-21-societal-myths

25   https://www.endviolenceagainstwomen.org.uk/wp-content/uploads/Data-tables-for-Attitudes-to-Sexual-Consent-research-report.pdf

British men (and 21% of women) believe that if a woman flirts while on a date with a man, then it isn't rape if he has sex with her without her consent. That means that if someone goes on a first date and is flirtatious over dinner, just about one in three men and one in five women believe that person has no right or ability to deny sex. If the victim doesn't give consent, then the dinner date hasn't done anything wrong and any complaint to the police is simply buyer's remorse, revenge or attention-seeking.

In addition, a third of men in the UK also think that once sex has started, a woman cannot withdraw consent and ask for it to stop. When a third of men think that women don't need to consent to sex when they've been flirting on a date, and a third think that a woman doesn't have the right to change her mind during sex, we begin to understand why rape victims are often not believed.[26] The fact of the matter is, however, that these examples are rape, legally. Whether or not we believe the rape victim, she has indeed been raped.

Let's think about it a different way. One in four

---

26 There is likely significant overlap between these two groups, but they are not necessarily all of the same people.

people in the UK believe that sex without consent inside a longer-term relationship isn't rape.[27] In fact, rape within marriage wasn't even a crime until 1991. Given this, perhaps it is not then hugely surprising that assaults by a current or former partner account for around two in five rapes in the UK.[28]

Put all this together and it means that a not insubstantial number of people don't believe that you have a choice about who you have sex with and when. And it's these beliefs that drive victims to remain silent, meaning that crimes go unreported and attitudes don't change. The result is a continued rape epidemic.

In May 2018, promoting her about-to-be released book *On Rape*, author Germaine Greer told a literary festival that, to her mind, most rape is just lazy or "bad sex". This caused a furore in the press,[29]

---

27   https://www.endviolenceagainstwomen.org.uk/wp-content/uploads/Data-tables-for-Attitudes-to-Sexual-Consent-research-report.pdf

28   https://www.ons.gov.uk/peoplepopulationandcommunity/crimeandjustice/articles/sexualoffendingvictimisation-andthepaththroughthecriminaljusticesystem/2018-12-13

29   https://www.nytimes.com/2018/05/31/world/europe/germaine-greer-rape.html

with people either loudly agreeing or disagreeing with her. She told the public that she'd been raped when she was younger, and that victims should stop carrying on about it – and that sentences for rape should be reduced to 200 hours of community service.

At the time, I accused her of just trying to sell more copies of her book. But the reality is, Greer was saying what a lot of people think. For some people, most of the time, rape seems to be more of a misunderstanding than a violation, and victims who make a fuss are doing it for the wrong reasons, such as revenge or attention-seeking.

Saying that rape is just bad sex is demeaning and belittles the impact it has on so many lives. Bad sex is embarrassing, but rape is often life altering. Bad sex becomes a story you tell with a laugh or a shake of the head, but rape victims suffer physically, emotionally and economically in ways that most people who haven't been through it simply don't understand.

Perhaps making it even more complicated, each rape victim reacts differently to the trauma and their reactions can even change over time. Understanding the trauma responses of one rape victim doesn't mean that you understand another's, or even that same victim's responses a year later. It makes it incredibly complicated for friends and families of victims to be sympathetic when they can't understand why someone is acting the way they are.

Almost all rape victims display trauma responses and trauma stress symptoms in the weeks following their assault. Approximately 50% of those victims go on to fully develop Post Traumatic Stress Disorder (PTSD).[30, 31] Symptoms of this disorder can include re-experiencing the trauma through flashbacks or nightmares, hypervigilance, anxiety, depression, numbing behaviours (like excessive extroversion, excessive introversion, overeating, undereating, alcohol and drug misuse and sexual promiscuity), avoidance, panic attacks, and more.[32]

---

30 https://www.ncbi.nlm.nih.gov/pmc/articles/PMC2323517/

31 For discussion around incorrect diagnosis of personality disorders and other mental illnesses based on the symptoms victims display after trauma rather than trauma itself being the cause of those symptoms, see Taylor, Jessica (2022). *Sexy But Psycho*. (Constable).

32 A non-exhaustive list of symptoms can be found here: https://www.nhs.uk/mental-health/conditions/post-traumatic-stress-disorder-ptsd/symptoms/

But PTSD isn't subjective: it can even be seen on an MRI scan.[33] It is also linked with an increase of certain cancers, fibromyalgia,[34] diabetes and heart disease.[35] Around one in three rape victims have suicidal thoughts and 13% go on to attempt suicide.[36] This differs hugely from the general population: rape victims are 13 times more likely to attempt suicide than women who haven't been a victim.[37] Bad sex, embarrassment, buyer's remorse, do not cause PTSD and suicide. Rape does.

Winnie, Emily J and I were all diagnosed with PTSD after being raped. For me, PTSD manifested in hyperventilating panic attacks, dissociation (when I couldn't get out of the trap of my own head and would be unable to move or speak), irrationality, hypervigilance (always alert to what was going on around me, so if I so much as walked down the street, I'd jump at every small sound, to the point

33   van der Kolk, B. A. (2014). *The body keeps the score: Brain, mind, and body in the healing of trauma.* (Viking).

34   https://pubmed.ncbi.nlm.nih.gov/29745889/

35   https://www.health.harvard.edu/diseases-and-conditions/past-trauma-may-haunt-your-future-health

36   https://mainweb-v.musc.edu/vawprevention/research/mentalimpact.shtml

37   *ibid.*

of daily exhaustion), drinking too much, reaching out to people who I knew thought I was worthless and so wouldn't help me, not eating, depression and anxiety. This isn't even an exhaustive list. Having never contemplated suicide before being raped, I was one of the 13% of victims who make a serious attempt to take their own lives. By the time I was diagnosed with PTSD 10 months after I was raped, I had imploded most of my personal and professional relationships. I was acting like a crazy person, because, frankly, that's exactly what I was. I had, for all intents and purposes, temporarily lost my mind. And for me, it started on the night I was raped with that hyperventilating panic attack and being treated like someone who was carrying on for no good reason, rather than someone who had been through a terrible ordeal.

Not long after my PTSD diagnosis, I was standing in a queue outside my daughter's primary school. She was in a school play and was very excited because not only was I coming, but so was my own mother. We stood outside in the sunshine while the bigger kids came through selling their newsletter to the parents. My daughter had been in the school since nursery and I knew the parents from her year, at least by sight. It was a bright and lovely day, there was nothing inherently stressful about the situation, but I realised that every single muscle in my body was tense and my eyes were darting around looking for danger like a cartoon spy. I must have looked like the world's most obvious robbery lookout. The only actual stress behind the physical symptoms was that I was having a difficult time with my ex-husband's family and was irrationally worried they'd turn up. But my mind and demeanour were that of someone under attack. While I was able to work to calm down, the rest of the day felt like nails on a chalkboard. I was deeply irritable and, soon, absolutely exhausted from my body's behaviour. At least the fact that I knew I had PTSD meant that I could in that moment recognise its impact. I had some tools to try and combat the symptoms, but they didn't help them to stop.

For Emily J, Winnie and me, PTSD meant the collapse of promising careers in mid-stride. The personal economic fallout we faced after being raped was dramatic and lasted for years. Indeed, academic studies have found that PTSD has substantial economic impacts, not only on the victim but on the "family, employer and wider society".[38] In a study of people who developed PTSD as a result of the 7/7 London bombings, there were clear economic losses due to the literal cost of treating PTSD but also the amount of sick leave required for each person (between 1 and 1,112 days) and the amount of time that people spent unemployed as a result of the condition (3 to 320 weeks).[39] PTSD can be sneaky and persistent. It stole the latter half of my 30s and it has stolen so much more from many more people.

About one in three people who suffer an extreme trauma develop PTSD[40] – and this is seen across a variety of studies, including victims of terrorism and people who have seen frontline combat during times of war.[41] For rape victims, however, it is one in two. In our earlier thought experiment counting

---

38   https://pureadmin.qub.ac.uk/ws/portalfiles/portal/181776919/ijpmh_raft1003.pdf

39   *ibid.*

40   https://www.nhs.uk/conditions/post-traumatic-stress-disorder-ptsd/causes/

41   https://neuro.psychiatryonline.org/doi/pdf/10.1176/jnp.16.2.135

sexual assault victims in a train carriage, this means that not only had eight women in the carriage been raped, but possibly four of them had gone on to develop PTSD as a result.

Rape victims are going through a level of trauma so extreme that it alters the brain chemistry of half of them, fundamentally changes their physical responses to stress, causes emotional distress and often economic destruction. Rape victims are being sent into combat against their wishes and their bodies are the battleground. But there's no coming home from this war, because we live inside the battleground even after the fighting is done. And what's more, society's attitudes towards rape mean that most of us can't even talk about it.

Not only the 10% of rape victims assaulted by a stranger experience PTSD. Not only the cut-and-dried, black-and-white cases. Not only the righteous victims who the police choose to believe, or who the prosecutors think are worth taking forward. This is what happens to 50% of rape victims, whether you believe they were raped or not.

Just as being in combat and not developing PTSD doesn't negate the reality of being in combat, neither does being raped and not developing PTSD. The rape victim who doesn't develop PTSD hasn't experienced anything less real or less valid – but I use the example of the 50% who do suffer from PTSD to show how real and persistent the effects of rape are; the disorder is a very real thing. This shows us that a rape victim's experience of rape isn't just a misunderstanding, or bad sex, or overreacting, or being vindictive, or any of the other lines used to excuse sex without consent. The victims' bodies have been so intimately violated and they've been rendered so powerless that half of them go on to develop PTSD.

Rape is real, prevalent and persistent. It changes lives – and it ends them. It has an enduring impact on the victim, their family, their employer and our whole society.

Chapter Three

A few years ago, my friend, Kat Araniello, was dating a man she'd met at a festival. He said he was a policeman and he seemed really lovely. He was thoughtful and kind, always doing little things for her without being asked. She was starting to daydream about a future with him.

Except it turned out that nothing he'd told her was true. Not only was he not a police officer, he had a string of previous convictions for assaulting women he'd been dating and had recently spent time in jail. One night he attacked Kat, threatening to kill her, using a knife to tear her clothes off and holding it to her neck while he raped her. He held her prisoner for days. When the police came – people who at the time she thought were her attacker's colleagues – she initially declined to formally report to them what had happened and was, in their opinion, "not the right kind of upset".

A few days later, Kat was able to stand up and file a police report. Her rapist was eventually charged by the CPS, but the week before the trial, they dropped the case. They said that the way Kat had acted on the night of the attack was a problem and that a jury wouldn't believe her. This was a man with previous convictions for domestic abuse, who had a fake warrant card and was impersonating a police officer. There was ample evidence of the attack – not least pictures of Kat with her battered body covered in bruises, along with her clothes shredded by the knife. But that was not enough. The CPS didn't trust a jury of men and women to understand that Kat was afraid for her life, scared, too, that the police who turned up at her door were her attacker's colleagues and friends, that she was suffering from severe trauma and that there is no "right" kind of upset after something like that. The CPS decided that a jury would not be capable of understanding that what had happened to Kat was rape and assault.

While rape is a serious crime with a huge impact on its victims, it's not generally treated like one. Unfortunately, as of early 2022, only around 1.3% of reported rapes in the UK resulted in the attacker being charged.[42]

Why is that?

In England and Wales, the police investigate a rape and put together the evidence before sending the file to the CPS; the CPS then decides whether or not to charge the suspect. A lot of things can go wrong along the way, even before the case reaches the CPS. There could be no witnesses or CCTV footage to corroborate the victim's story. The police could have trouble securing evidence; in my case, for example, the police were unable to obtain CCTV evidence from the bar where I'd supposedly met John because they waited too long and by the time they requested it, it simply didn't exist anymore. But if the police do feel there is sufficient evidence, they send a summary of the case to the CPS, which then makes the decision whether or not to take the case forward.

---

42   https://www.independent.co.uk/news/uk/crime/rape-prosecutions-charges-england-wales-b2001818.html

The CPS are legally required to look at two things: whether there is a reasonable chance of conviction (51% or more) and if the prosecution is in the public interest. And it's this decision-making process which means that in 98.7% of all rape cases reported to the police, either the police or the CPS decide not to take the case forward against the alleged offender.

I believe that a fundamental reason why rape is so prevalent is because it so often goes unprosecuted, for reasons ranging from victims' complicated responses to trauma, to it being a crime that is inherently difficult to prosecute. Another important factor, however, is a widespread belief amongst the public, the police and prosecutors in rape myths.

The CPS's thinking in refusing to take Kat's attacker to trial because they didn't think a jury would easily believe her was not entirely wrong. There has been quite a bit of academic research into the impact of rape myths on how police, prosecutors and even juries decide whether someone has been raped or not. Rape myths are the stereotypes, prejudices and false beliefs that, consciously or not, generally shift the blame from the perpetrator to the victim.

Rape myths include: that a woman brought it on herself; that women lie about rape; that women who wear provocative clothing or who are drinking alcohol are asking for it; that flirting means you don't need consent for sex; and so on. They are all thoughts in our heads that provide excuses or reasons why something isn't really rape, or why we don't believe a woman who says she's been raped. Some of them may have already formed in your own head when you read earlier about Kat, Emily J or me. But let's be clear: rape myths are exactly that. Myths. Even the CPS itself has previously admitted that at least 98% of the time, when someone says they've been raped, they've been raped,[43] and a similar study from the Home Office puts it at 97%[44] of the time.

Nevertheless, a recent analysis of previously published academic research on jury decision-making in rape cases, showed that belief in rape myths will colour the way that

---

43 By coincidence, not long after I started quoting this CPS study in the press, it disappeared from their website.
44 https://www.researchgate.net/publication/238713283_ Home_Office_Research_Study_293_A_gap_or_a_chasm_ Attrition_in_reported_rape_cases

juries evaluate evidence, and can even influence their decision-making.[45] And not only by a little. Academics have proven that two people looking at exactly the same evidence come to different conclusions about whether someone is guilty of rape – and that difference can be accurately predicted based on their responses to an abstract rape-myth scale[46, 47].

However, this is a fixable problem. Further research has shown that if a judge's instructions to a jury include education on rape myths and why they aren't true, they are more likely to convict a

---

45   Leverick, F. (2020) "What do we know about rape myths and juror decision making?" *International Journal of Evidence and Proof.*
46   *ibid.*
47   The existence and impact of rape myths on juries is widely regarded as a question of "how much" and "how to address" the issue, not if it is a real phenomenon. However, as a counterpoint, there is one academic dissenter to this point of view. Cheryl Thomas believes that her research shows that jurors essentially become better versions of themselves and drop their beliefs in rape myths while serving on a jury (oddly, even while serving on a jury in a case involving any sort of crime, in other words while serving on a jury that has nothing to do with rape). For a detailed discussion of the flaws of Thomas's research please see https://repository.lboro.ac.uk/articles/journal_contribution/ Myths_about_myths_A_commentary_on_Thomas_2020_ and_the_question_of_jury_rape_myth_acceptance/16559307

rapist.[48] Perhaps one of the greatest reasons for hope in the last few years comes from the conviction of Harvey Weinstein for rape in February 2020. This case was complicated and included victims who didn't behave the way society often assumes rape victims should, such as continuing to associate with Weinstein and even, in one case, having consensual sex with him even though he had previously raped her. The defence made a great deal out of this. But the jury saw through it all, showing that it is entirely possible to help juries overcome their innate belief in rape myths.

My central argument is that it's vital we start prosecuting more rape cases, not least because if rapists get away with it once, so many will go on to do it again and again. On average, they commit rape 5.8 times over the course of their lives.[49] For every reported rape that does not result in a prosecution, there is a greater than coin-toss chance that that rapist will go on to do it again. By not

---

48   Leverick, F. (2020) "What do we know about rape myths and juror decision making?" *International Journal of Evidence and Proof.*

49   "Repeat rape and multiple offending among undetected rapists" https://www.documentcloud.org/documents/1699822-2002-lisak-repeatrapeinundetectedrapists.html

prosecuting rape, we let this continue, with more and more women each year being attacked by someone who should already be in jail.

Unfortunately, seemingly cowed by a small number of high-profile cases in which it was claimed the offender had been falsely accused, the CPS has taken the opposite approach. Instead of pursuing more rape cases and educating juries to set aside their prejudices, they have steadfastly doubled down on not prosecuting rape. Moreover, in 2016, the CPS began operating an unofficial target system of not taking rape cases forward unless prosecutors felt they were at least 60% winnable in front of a jury – more than the 51% reasonable chance of conviction they are required to test cases against.[50] A whistleblower brought the existence of this unofficial target to light. It's generally assumed that this target was created because a higher conviction rate for cases that made it to court would be better for the CPS's reputation. Contrary to CPS claims, however, research from an Oxford professor shows that this likely led to a dramatic drop in the number

---

50   https://www.theguardian.com/society/2019/nov/13/
secret-cps-targets-may-have-led-to-cases-being-dropped

of rapists being charged,[51] even though rape reports increased dramatically during that time.[52]

While, obviously, rape myths and the difficulty in securing evidence for rapes do contribute to the fact that it is a deeply under-prosecuted crime, it is also part of a wider trend of plummeting prosecution rates. We now have a criminal justice system that sometimes seems to be intent on not protecting its victims. Only 6% of reported crimes in the UK result in someone being charged,[53] a number that has been falling steadily for years.

Eight years ago, I was out having drinks with a friend at a bar in Shoreditch. I, along with a few other people, had piled jackets and bags on a corner couch. A couple I didn't know started having a giant, screaming row right near that couch and everyone subtly started moving away. That was an error. The entire thing was a set-up. The couple

---

51   https://static1.squarespace.com/static/5aa98420f2e6b-1ba0c874e42/t/5efa253734314d7760c7a50e/1593451864833/Volume+10+redacted.pdf

52   The modelling from Professor Adams also, crucially, disproves the notion that the drop in rape prosecutions is linked to reductions in police resources.

53   https://www.independent.co.uk/news/uk/crime/rape-prosecutions-charges-england-wales-b2001818.html

grabbed my laptop bag and ran out. The police were called – they turned up immediately, interviewed me and everyone else, looked at the CCTV footage and swiftly got a copy of the credit card receipt the couple had used to pay for their drinks. It was probably 10 days later when the police rang me to say that the couple had been arrested, that my bag hadn't been recovered and would I prefer to see them put on trial to possibly end up jailed, or for them to be cautioned, pay me for my losses and apologise. I took the second option.

More recently, in spring 2019, my phone was stolen out of my hand by a man on a bicycle in broad daylight in front of a popular restaurant in Bermondsey – and my experience could not have been more different. The police weren't interested in speaking to me about it and I was told to fill in an online form to report the crime, to obtain a crime number for insurance purposes. After a couple of weeks, someone turned on my phone briefly and I let the police know the location. When I followed up to see if they'd had any luck tracking down my phone, it turned out that when they checked their online CCTV system, they didn't find any obvious nearby camera feeds and had dropped the case. They hadn't even rung the restaurant to ask if they had CCTV. The police weren't remotely apologetic, nor did they seem to think it was their job to investigate the brazen theft of something worth hundreds of pounds.

I often say that rape has been almost effectively decriminalised in the UK, but it's also true to say that crime more generally no longer attracts the same attention from police and prosecutors as before. This was not always the case for criminality as a whole, and it was not, at one time, true of sexual offences. So perhaps if I'd been raped a few years earlier, my experience with the police and the CPS would have been different. But whatever the truth, considering the life-altering impact of rape and the serial nature of the criminals who rape women, we urgently need to consider what could possibly be in the public interest of only pursuing a prosecution in 1.3% of reported rapes.

Chapter Four

"The Crown Prosecution Service, in its infinite wisdom, did a study," I began, looking out over a sea of about 60 faces, most of whom I'd never met before. I was standing on the small stage of a co-working office in East London on an October evening in 2017. I gripped the microphone tightly in my right hand, trying not to show how nervous I was. It was a rare night out for me and I was at a public speaking group where I was supposed to be working on my nerves by giving a minute-long talk on "Parenting tips from my seven-year-old daughter". I was dressed in a slinky black top that I almost never had cause to wear, for drinks at the pub afterwards with my friend Sarah. My daughter was away for half term with her dad for the first time, and I was having a week off from being a full-time single mother. I was out, at night, without a babysitter, for the first time in ages.

"In this study," I continued, trying to focus on the individuals in the audience one by one rather than the expanse of strangers, "they were trying to find out about the scourge of false rape accusations. And they found out that it's true: 2–6%[54] of the time, when a woman says she's been raped, she's lying. That means that 94–98% of the time, if a woman says she's been raped, she's telling the truth. Does anybody know what the conviction rate is for rape? In London it's in single digits. Think about that for a moment."

I paused. I definitely hadn't started my day knowing what was going to come next. But it was time.

That morning, I'd been sitting in a sleek photographic gallery's cafe in West London, sipping coffee and catching up with a former client, Camilla.[55] I'd done a huge research project for her

---

54 This is actually incorrect. I'd conflated two studies. The CPS study found that 98% of the time, if a woman says she's been raped, then she's been raped. Globally, it's usually 90–98% of the time.

55 Some names have been changed for privacy.

the previous year, going around the country speaking with people about how they felt about life and their mobile phones. It had been a lot of fun and Camilla had been great to work with. But I'd never really explained why I'd stopped being in contact or where I'd been for the last year. As I told her what had happened to me, not just at the Town Hall Hotel in May 2015, but everything that had – and hadn't – happened since, Camilla nodded along. As I paused and took another sip of coffee, she looked at me.

"You know that I'm a magistrate, right?" she began. I sort of remembered but hadn't really understood what it meant.

"A magistrate is a lay judge, we make decisions in court," she explained.

I nodded.

"And, every few years," Camilla continued, "we get a letter from the government asking us to send fewer people to jail."

I stared at her in disbelief, my heart racing as I tried to digest what she was saying. As my horror grew at what this meant, something small inside me snapped.

Chapter Four

I had started off that day assuming that I'd be speaking for a minute on my daughter's parenting tips, but all day long I couldn't shake a rising anger. My case didn't go forward because the police didn't do their jobs, because the CPS doesn't want to prosecute difficult cases, because the courts don't want to send people to jail. Only it was worse. The whole system seemed disinclined to send criminals to jail or hold anyone to account. I had lost control of my body to John, lost my power to the police, but even more so, the entire system made it impossible for a victim. I'd ended up fighting the system instead of the system fighting for me. I never had a chance.

When the head of the speaking group pointed at me and said that I had five minutes to speak instead of one, I felt like there was only one thing I could do. I had to stand on that stage and try to change things.

"My name is Emily Hunt and I'm standing up here because about two years ago I woke up naked in a hotel bed next to somebody I'd never seen before."

As I told my story, the audience leant forward in their seats. You could have heard a pin drop. But the point of standing on that stage and talking about what had happened to me wasn't to get it off my chest. I wanted something. Help to crowdfund the private prosecution of my rapist, for a start. At the end of those five most difficult, raw and exposed minutes of my life, talking about the worst thing that had ever happened to me in front of more than 100 prying eyes, not only did the strangers sitting in that audience clap, but they came up to me and asked where my sign-up sheet was. They asked what they could do to help. They said I gave them hope. They said I could change the world.

My friend Sarah hugged me as I collapsed into my seat, drained. When journalists started calling a few days later, I realised that the people from the audience might be right. Maybe I really could change something. After so many false starts and disappointments, after each small hope for justice was destroyed through inaction, maybe there really was something to hope for now – because for the first time, I wasn't entirely alone in the fight. I had hundreds of people at my back, rooting for me, supporting me and carrying that hope for me.

But it wasn't always clear that this was the way things were going to go.

Chapter Four

The support and the advice given to rape victims is often provided by a disparate collection of organisations from the voluntary sector. In the days and weeks after I was raped, I knew that I wasn't okay. I couldn't breathe, I couldn't eat, I couldn't think straight. Reaching out for help was nearly impossible, but when I got desperate enough and scared enough at the way my thoughts were circling ceaselessly in my mind, I picked up the phone and tried to find support.

I sat in my bedroom with my laptop open, the lights out and the blind pulled down. In the darkness, I stared at the open browser tab and tried to ring one organisation listed on a webpage, only to be told that I wasn't in their catchment area. They gave me a different number to call. I rang it and it went to a voicemail message that suggested a different number. I called that one and they said they weren't able to help at that time and gave me a different organisation to call. As I entered the next number in my phone, I realised that it was the first number I'd called nearly an hour earlier. I'd been in a full circle. I put down my phone. Staring at the ceiling and unable to move, I'd never felt more alone.

Often, when we talk about rape or sexual violence, it's as though they are ideas strictly reserved for discussion within the sphere of "women's issues", rather than treating sexual violence as a serious, life-altering crime that directly impacts one in five women and one in twenty-five men,[56] as well as countless families, friends and even employers. Even though rape can and does happen to anyone, any discussion is more often than not pigeonholed as something that feminists do, or something that only liberals and lefties talk about. The infrastructure for supporting victims of rape is, perhaps unsurprisingly then, largely volunteer-based and through organisations that often identify with a cause or a movement.

The voluntary sector has done a huge amount to help countless victims, myself included – and this should not be diminished in any way. But supporting rape victims is treated as an optional extra in our society, something that volunteers should deal with, as if rape is somehow elective. As though victims could choose not be raped. It leads to a vicious cycle.

---

56   https://rapecrisis.org.uk/get-informed/statistics-sexual-violence/

Chapter Four

We know that 90% of rape victims are women, but that doesn't make rape "just a women's issue". Because supporting rape victims has been largely delegated to the women's sector, however, public discourse on rape often ends up occurring in a silo. People with left-leaning politics and self-identified feminists dominate the conversation, which largely occurs only within their political sphere. Occasionally, soundbites escape into the mainstream. While these organisations are doing hugely valuable and laudable work, this environment limits the way people outside that sphere understand and talk about rape and sexual violence.

For example, imagine an extreme left-wing feminist organisation[57] that supports rape victims in a small town. They would be greatly needed by the community they serve to provide things like post-rape counselling and support, as it's likely they'd be the only organisation that could provide that support locally and in person to the communities that need it. But it wouldn't be surprising if an organisation with that sort of leaning would

---

57 This is a hypothetical thought experiment and I have no actual organisation in mind.

proclaim publicly that men are the problem, and the cause of rape and other violence against women. The fact of the matter is, they wouldn't be wrong in saying that. The way that rape laws are written in England and Wales, only a man can be a rapist. This is problematic in two ways.

First, it allows some organisations to implicitly lump all men into this category, suggesting that all men have the capacity to be rapists. In fact, maybe 6% of men are rapists,[58] meaning that nearly 19 out of 20 are not. Stigmatising men as a whole is another reason rape isn't talked about and attitudes don't change.

Second, it contributes towards pigeonholing rape as a women's issue, rather than one that affects the whole of society. As a result, support is often given to victims on an *ad hoc* and non-professional basis, delivered by well-meaning women's groups, excusing large sections of society from talking about it. That leaves rape victims in the position I was in: alone, suffering and with no hope.

Rape is not a women's issue. It is a human issue.

---

58 "Repeat rape and multiple offending among undetected rapists" https://www.documentcloud.org/documents/1699822-2002-lisak-repeatrapeinundetectedrapists.html

* * *

Ten months after I was raped, I sat on a double bed in a hotel room with high ceilings and huge windows. Light poured in over me as I typed on my laptop. I'd taken a shower, changed into my pyjamas and poured myself a glass of champagne. With my hair still wet and clinging to my top, I finished a long email to my best friend from graduate school.

Gabe had been my "man of honour" at my wedding. We'd been close for more than a decade. In my email, I wrote about how, in the previous 10 months, the police had treated me horribly from beginning to end. I wrote about how every interaction with them had been deeply traumatising. I wrote about what it felt like to not be believed, to be dismissed, viewed as a crank or a burden, someone in it for attention. I wrote about feeling lost and alone. I wrote about having lost my sense of self. I wrote about putting a note in my daughter's ballet kit that morning telling her that I loved her before I sent her off on a two-night-long sleepover at a friend's house. I wrote that they should tell her that I died in a car accident. I wrote that I was done, that I was ready to go, that the only way the police wouldn't treat anyone ever again the way they treated me was if they were forced to learn their lesson. I wrote that I was sorry for not being strong enough. I wrote that I was dying as a result of what happened that May night as sure as if I'd actually died on that night.

I hit send.

Then I forwarded the email to two police officers who I felt were particularly responsible for the horrible way that I'd been treated and the fact that I'd never see justice for what had happened to me. I sent it to those two because I felt like they'd contributed the most to breaking me down little by little in the months after the rape. I shut my laptop. It was time. I was sitting on a double bed in a light-filled room in the middle of the day at the Town Hall Hotel. The same hotel where I'd been raped. And then I started swallowing pills.

The week before, the police had finally released a copy of the toxicology report to me. I'd been asking for it for months. It had become a sort of totem to me, for no reason really, other than that I needed some data to make sense of everything. Or perhaps just to make sense of anything.

When the report finally arrived attached to an email in my inbox, the lab technician's name was blacked out to protect their privacy, but pretty much everything else was on the report. As I started to skim through it, I wasn't expecting there to be anything particularly interesting or illuminating. I just wanted to understand. But then the world swam in front of me. Words started to collapse into each other. I stopped reading. I stopped breathing. I couldn't move. I had found both the reason my case hadn't gone forward and the reason it absolutely should have.

In the neatly typed text on the form report were two bombshells. The first was that the police had given the wrong timeline to the toxicology lab for analysing my urine sample; as a result, their conclusive finding that I hadn't been drugged was wrong. But the second was the biggest for me in that moment. The second bombshell was that my attacker had been stone-cold sober and had been arrested while in possession of drugs he said were Viagra and LSD. Even one of these two facts would have been devastating. Together, it wasn't just a punch to the gut: it was more. It was life shattering. Life ending.

Finally having the toxicology report in my hands made me feel like I had proof that the police had decided that I didn't exist, and that perhaps I shouldn't. In the throes of an undiagnosed PTSD crisis, I'd sent my suicide letter to the police, hoping that they'd finally see that I'd been a victim worthy of their work and in the hope that no other victim would be treated the way I had been. It was irrational – my death wouldn't have impacted the police in any way whatsoever – but, in my fractured mind, it was the only way to have an impact and change anything.

I didn't want the world to be the way it was, and I felt like leaving it was the only thing I could do.

My phone started to ring and I didn't answer it. I had another sip of champagne and my eyes were drifting closed. The pills were working and I was feeling very little, truly at peace for the first time in a long while, until my mind drifted to my daughter. At my insistence, my ex-husband had moved out of the house at the end of the summer, about three or four months after I'd been raped. I'd started a new job that September and was surprised and hurt when he stopped helping with childcare. The one time he was supposed to pick her up from school in the months after he moved out, he was running so late that I had to rush to the school to collect her. Suddenly I was trying to juggle school runs and a big job at a PR agency, and while it was bumpy, my daughter and I had been getting used to it being just us. We still had breakfast together in bed in the mornings and I had a few friends who were helping us with school pick-ups when I couldn't get there in time. But the reality was that I wasn't just breaking, I was broken.

The weight of PTSD pushed down on me every day. As I was writing my suicide letter to my friend Gabe, I genuinely thought that someone else would be better at raising my daughter than I was at that point. Everything was hard for me. I could barely eat; small things stressed me out to the point of not being able to move and so the big things would send my mind reeling in directions I couldn't come back from. I was working at barely 10–15% of my capacity at my new job. As a parent, I had no patience – not because of my daughter, but because the world just felt impossible. Most of those long summer days, the sunlight walking home from school in the park felt too bright; it felt like it had weight to it that added to the burden pushing me further down every day. Nothing I did made life feel even a little bit doable. When the pile of my unopened post grew too big, I moved it unopened to a drawer by the front door. I couldn't even muster the energy to open an envelope, let alone figure out what to do with the contents.

But as I shifted on the bed and felt the cool hotel linen under my hands, I remembered the morning after I was raped, when my daughter kissed my nose. How, when my daughter was in the hospital as a toddler and was extremely ill and they didn't know why, I had fought like a lioness to keep her safe and get her well. I remembered how I had filled her bookshelves with books to help her mind grow. I filled her body with the best food I could find. I held her and protected her and cheered for every skinned knee and every ripped pair of tights because kids should get dirty while playing in the park. I thought about every screen-time limit and every story read at bedtime. I thought about every hand held, every conversation had over breakfast, every laugh, every tear.

In that moment of sudden lucidity, I knew that no one would ever love my daughter as much as I do, or as well as I do. No one would ever put her first the way I do. No one would ever take care of her the way I do. No one else would ever put all they have into helping her live the best possible life she could.

Like lightning it cracked through my mind: no matter my flaws, no matter how imperfect I am, I am her mother. No one else will ever be that. I cannot do this to her. I cannot leave her.

Obviously, a lot of things went wrong in the days, weeks and months after I was raped. I was failed by the criminal justice system, by a lack of support from the police and the medical system and by a fragmented voluntary sector doing the best it could.

But in the time since, I've realised that one of the hardest things to deal with as a rape victim was the fact the people either didn't believe that I'd been raped or believed that I should stop carrying on and that it can't have been so bad as to cause PTSD – or something in between.

The thing is, I think this reaction is entirely human. Rape is genuinely horrible. As discussed in Chapter Two, rape causes PTSD at a substantially higher rate than other traumatic events, including living through combat and terrorist attacks. On a gut level, it makes sense that people would have a hard time dealing with the idea that someone they know, or even just someone they know of, has been violated in this way. It probably makes it worse that what happened to me could have happened to anyone, because to follow that thought process through means it could happen to them or to someone they love.

But we can go a step further. Research shows people who believe that we live in a more-or-less just world are more likely to believe in rape myths[59] and, essentially, find reasons to blame a rape victim for what has happened to them rather than the rapist. For someone who thinks that the world is more-or-less an okay place, that good things happen to good people and people get what they deserve, the reaction to being confronted with something different – like someone being raped – is to cling to their fundamental belief that the world is a just place, meaning they will essentially have to discount the rape victim.

In the days and weeks after I was raped, I was

---

59 https://journals.sagepub.com/doi/10.1177/
0886260514549196

having a hard time breathing. For the first time in my life, I was suffering from hyperventilating panic attacks and felt like someone was sitting on my chest. I was living a repeat of the night I was raped, unable to catch my breath as I dragged air in at a frantic pace, afraid that my chest would collapse under the weight of the effort to get oxygen.

I'd done a fair amount of Pilates over the previous few years and had become friends with the owner of a local Pilates and yoga studio, a man called Luke.[60] I'd been on a few of his retreats and even ended up doing his studio's yoga teacher training. None of what I'd learned in the classes, training or retreats was helping me cope. I'd spent months of Sundays sitting in Luke's small studio during our yoga teacher training, listening to hawkers selling their flowers outside before dawn while he guided us all through a meditation or a breathing exercise.

---

60 Some names and details have been changed. "Luke" isn't a person to be recognised here, or called out, or named and shamed. Like many stories of my feeling let down by people, this is about the broader picture of how people can discount the experiences of rape victims, and that it's a normal human response. But it's one we need to tackle and do better on, on an individual level.

Now I couldn't find that kind of calm, or any calm, really. I couldn't find my breath. I needed help.

I reached out to him, my teacher and friend, and asked if he could do some breathing exercises or guided meditation with me. I'd been forced to tell him what had happened as he was one of the nearly half a dozen local friends I'd called and left messages for that night from the hospital. When I had to explain the next day why I'd called and what the meaning of my message was, I felt forced to tell him that I'd been raped.

But we never found a time to meet up or even for him to talk me through a guided breathing exercise on the phone. I was so disorientated and hurt from my experience, that I don't think I particularly noticed how odd it seemed at that time of crisis to have asked for help and not received it.

A few months later, I heard through the grapevine that Luke essentially thought I was being overly dramatic about my experience – that realisation really stung. But the reality is, he wouldn't have been the only one in my life to feel that way. Not even close. I've heard similar stories from other victims.

The most important aspect of this sort of reaction – discounting a victim's experience, not believing them or trying to find ways to shift the blame to them in some way – is that they probably didn't understand their own reactions. It has almost nothing to do with the victim or their story. For example, for someone like Luke, with a female partner, sisters and lots of female friends and clients, what is easier to contemplate? That a woman could be drugged and raped while out at an innocuous lunch in a local restaurant with her father, or that a woman could be over-egging a bad night out? It seemed as if Luke, who otherwise prides himself on kindness and community and believes that the world is a good place, had at best, on reflex, engaged in victim blaming, or, at worst, perhaps believed I'd made the whole thing up. However, his reaction is completely in line with the academic research on how people with a just world view deal with rape.

This all-too-human reaction is taking place not just in response to what happened to me in May 2015, but to other rape victims every day. It is one of the reasons why victims don't break their silence or wait years before doing so. But the worst aspect of this is that rape victims aren't believed or feel like they won't be believed, even though false rape allegations are so rare as to barely exist. Global estimates put the incidence of false rape allegations at 2–10%.[61] In the UK, as mentioned, this is more likely closer to 2–3%. But even when rape is falsely alleged, it is rarer still for the motive to be malicious or to pervert the course of justice. In a review, the CPS discovered that false rape allegations were deliberately made with the intention of perverting the course of justice in only 0.3% of cases.[62]

Imagine again that train carriage from Chapter Two, or looking around your office or thinking about the women in your life. If you know five or more women, you probably know at least one victim of sexual violence. There could be many reasons why none of them has told you that they've been raped, but it's quite possible they think you won't believe them. At the end of the day, no matter what one's personal position or feelings are, if told

---

61   https://web.archive.org/web/20180101025446/https://icdv.idaho.gov/conference/handouts/False-Allegations.pdf
62   https://qz.com/980766/the-truth-about-false-rape-accusations/

that someone has been raped, statistically speaking, they have been. And even though that goes against our internal wiring, it's time to confront it head on.

The flip side of this scenario is also true. Not only is it human nature to not believe a rape victim, it's also human nature, for many of the same reasons, to believe that someone who has been accused of rape has been falsely accused. Coming back to the statistics, in the UK, if you know 50 men who have been accused of rape, one or two of them might not be guilty. That's it. The other 48 or 49 definitely are.

Fundamentally, rape is violent and horrible, so if someone we know has been accused of rape it is entirely human to believe them when they say they haven't done it. Perhaps we need to believe that a woman has done something to cause the situation, or that it wasn't actually rape, because otherwise it's too horrible to think about.

When we watch TV crime shows, we can sort of understand murder. Obviously none of us would ever commit it, but we can understand it. Hundreds of different motives, justified or not, are shown to us every night in gritty shows: robbery gone wrong, power plays, revenge, jealousy, and so on. But rape is never really understandable in the same way. It's used in fiction to move the story along in a certain direction, to create tension or trauma, build a story arc or allow a character to develop. But we never root for a rapist, even a little bit. Even in the abstract, even in the safe fictional world happening on our screens, rape doesn't make sense. How could a reasonable person just accept its prevalence when not confronted by it personally, viscerally, unavoidably?

We each have to make a choice to simply believe.

Around the time I was regretting the 40 or so pills I'd swallowed and started reaching out for help, the police obtained a warrant to trace my phone. After receiving my email, they'd broken down the bright blue front door of my little house and not found me there. When they saw my approximate location from the trace on my phone, someone on the police force put two and two together and immediately understood where I was and why.

They wheeled me out on a stretcher and I left the hotel for the hospital in an ambulance, repeating the same journey I had taken that night 10 months earlier. But this time everything was different.

Chapter Four

Now I wanted to live. Now I wanted to, needed to, change my story.

A few weeks after my suicide attempt, I sat in a psychiatrist's office, talking with him at length about what had happened to me the previous year. He sat behind a large old dark wooden desk, taking notes by hand. The sounds of occasional traffic on Harley Street came up through the giant windows as light filtered in, dappled by the shadows of leafy trees. As he explained PTSD to me and went through a raft of treatment options, he stopped for a moment and looked me straight in the eyes.

"What you need more than a good therapist – and you *do* need a good therapist – is a lawyer," he said. "I know someone who might be able to help. She's a family friend."

I finally felt heard. I finally had hope.

Chapter Five

When I stood on that stage in October 2017 and bared my soul, if I'd known all of the twists and turns it would take, to be discounted over and over again, how much of my life it would take up, I *probably* would still have done it.

But I might not have.

I'd stood on that stage and announced my intention to try to change the world, even in a small way. I wanted to bring the first crowdfunded private rape prosecution in the UK. I wanted to make justice accessible to victims who were shut out of a criminal justice system that seemed not to understand that rapists belonged in front of a jury. But I had no support, I had no legal team, I just had my huge need to do something about it all, to take control back, to make something come of it all.

While a few people offered to help in various limited ways, I was still so much in the throes of PTSD that I couldn't see straight, let alone make good decisions. I no longer had the money to see a therapist and I spent days at a time hidden away, pulled to a thousand pieces by the stress of just needing to do something – and feeling supremely unsupported. I sat in my darkened bedroom with the curtain drawn against the light, as far under my duvet as possible, watching my phone blink on and glow as dozens of journalists rang me. I didn't have the energy to speak to anyone, and so just went to sleep. And then, there was Matthew Smith.

Matthew Smith, a mid-career barrister in Leeds, saw my story in the press and sent me a message out of the blue in early November 2017, offering to take up my case at no cost to me. If we won, he'd try to recoup his costs from the Crown on the basis that they should have prosecuted John in the first place.

Even before I met him in person, I trusted him. He seemed to genuinely care, to want to right this wrong. He asked intelligent questions and seemed deftly capable, able to understand when I was having trouble. I sent him all of the documents I had, and made sure that he had the CCTV footage, the video that John took of me, the summary of John's statement, the toxicology, everything I had or knew how to get. The police were being obstructive and refusing to give me any other evidence, but Matthew received everything he asked me for.

I took the train to Leeds on a cold and brisk January morning. Sitting across a dark, gleaming, wooden conference table from me, his laptop open, Matthew methodically went through the evidence in the case. No one had ever laid it all out for me before. I'd never wanted to read the notes from John's police interview, but Matthew read out a few sections to me to get my response and to hear my side.

"He says that as you were sleeping, he masturbated onto the bed and your thigh, and that he was holding your hand, but it's a bit unclear what that means," said Matthew.

"I'm sorry, what?"

"It's unclear if he was using your hand to masturbate himself; we ideally would have the transcript of his interview rather than this note," Matthew said, thinking that my question was about my hand.

"No, I'm sorry, did you just say that he admitted to masturbating onto my thigh?"

"Yes, it's right here," and Matthew proceeded to read out the section from the interview summary. I went ashen and was quiet for a moment.

"Matthew," I started, "the CPS specifically told me that the police had misspoken and that he hadn't masturbated onto me. I have the minutes of the meeting they sent to me; they were very clear, they told me he did not masturbate onto me."

"He did."

By the end of our long meeting and having gone through the evidence, Matthew felt that the case had merit.

"For me," he said when I asked him what he thought made it worth going forward, "it comes down to the video. I cannot emphasise this enough: it's very creepy."

He was clear that it was a difficult case though, as the toxicology didn't show definitively that I'd been drugged, and consent cases are by their nature difficult. He wanted time to review the evidence a bit more and look into a few things, so I left Leeds feeling positive but without a definite way forward.

However, at our next meeting, when Matthew said the words "realistic prospect of conviction", and that the case could go forward, I felt the world explode inside my head. Finally, finally John would be prosecuted and something would come from all of this. But Matthew wanted to bring on board a QC, a more senior, specialist lawyer who had experience in prosecuting a case like this, and so we would have to wait a bit longer.

In my memory, the amount of time that elapsed between Matthew saying he felt like there was a realistic prospect of conviction and the QC issuing his formal advice to the contrary feels like years. The fact is, I met with Matthew in January and the QC quashed the case in June. In total, I spent just under five months thinking that we were on track, that any day now the team would file the paperwork to charge John with rape. But every single one of those days that passed without that happening was deeply traumatic, in a way that no one seemed to understand.

Rape victims often speak about how afterwards, whether they chose to report the crime to the police or not, the feeling of being completely and totally not in control of one's own life is hugely destabilising. For me, from the moment the police turned up and started treating me like someone not worth listening to, I had no control over the crime that had happened to me, nor over what would come next. Standing on that stage and beginning the process of the private prosecution gave me glimpses of control, of power, of taking back my own life from all the people who had stolen it from me in all those small moments of not listening, not going forward, not considering how it felt to be living through it. And, of course, taking my life back from John, who almost stole it all that one night. He was the sole reason my power had been taken from me in all these ways, big or small.

Originally, I was told that the QC would need about three weeks to go through the evidence and give his advice. It took months longer than expected, with each new deadline passing with no real understanding of what it was doing to me. I'd been getting better with each step forward and each bit of control in my life that I won back, but I now fell back into a shell of myself; I sunk. Friendships I'd fought to build after my breakdown disintegrated; opportunities that had opened to me swiftly shut and I was barely able to move. I have almost no memories of that time, and it's like looking through gauze into a dim room, trying to pick out the shape of things and failing.

While waiting for the QC's decision, my mind fell into every trap that PTSD laid out for me. The delay felt purposeful, like he was stalling. Irrational thoughts crept in daily. Ideas spun through my mind: he was not the right person for the case, perhaps he hated women. Maybe it was all a set-up; his loyalty was to the CPS, who just wanted me and my case to go away. Maybe John's family were involved and were keeping the QC from moving forward. Spinning ideas, all of which I knew weren't true, filled the spaces between my thoughts. The reality is, no one treats victims the way they should be treated; there was no malice, just a total lack of compassion and understanding for what it feels like to be a victim of a crime who has been completely let down by the system and who is desperate to make something come of the experience.

It is, perhaps, a good thing that hope once found proved difficult to kill. On May 3, 2018 – nearly three years after I woke up in that hotel bed next to John – I sat across a scuffed conference table from Kate Ellis, the newest young solicitor to join the team at the Centre for Women's Justice. In the previous year and a half, I'd worked with two solicitors and spoken with at least four barristers in my attempt to see justice served. Every single one of them had let me down. Kate, however, was different.

Maybe it was because I'd been made redundant nearly 18 months before and hadn't spent much time sitting in offices since then, but the light in the conference room in the Pro Bono Centre on Chancery Lane was so brilliant in its fluorescence that my eyes hurt.

"You know," said Kate, her precise long blonde bob swinging just above the shoulders of her black blazer, "there's nothing stopping you from filing a new police report on just the video." She paused. "Then the police would have to consider the video on its own."

I had been explaining to Kate about the delay in the QC deciding whether or not to proceed with a private prosecution for rape, and that I felt nervous and stuck, with nothing going forward in the case.

"Before," she continued, "you had to trust that the CPS was correct that it wasn't illegal to take a video of someone naked without their consent, but your work with the government has proven otherwise."

Since I'd gone public with my rape in an effort to raise money to bring a private prosecution against John, I'd used some of the press coverage of my efforts to open doors with a few MPs. To my mind, the idea that it wasn't already illegal to video someone naked without their permission was mind boggling, and absolutely had to change. In the previous few months, I'd spoken with MPs from five different parties and was working towards a broad coalition of supporters to change the law, to make what happened to me illegal.

It was exciting to get to sit in MPs' offices and talk about not just what had happened to me, but what could change. In the midst of all of those meetings and that coalition-building, however, I'd received what seemed like an incredibly strange letter from the government. The Minister for

Chapter Five

Digital had consulted with the Solicitor General and the Ministry for Justice and they were adamant: the government could not support my campaign to make this sort of behaviour illegal, because to their minds, it already was. To the government, while they couldn't comment on my particular case, a situation like John's video of me seemed to be straightforward voyeurism, covered under the Sexual Offences Act of 2003.

John had admitted to every aspect of the crime of voyeurism as it was written in the 2003 law. He took the naked video of me without my permission, and he took it for future personal sexual gratification. He'd admitted that to the police under caution. To seek a prosecution on these grounds was an intriguing idea.

I decided to wait until the QC returned his much-overdue advice before making any decisions; it was finally dropped on me the following month. First, it was a long, carefully written document laying out, yet again, all of the ways in which I was not a worthy victim and that it would not be advisable to bring a private prosecution for rape, but that he would consider bringing a case for voyeurism. Although I wanted to go ahead immediately, there was, as always, an interminable pause and nothing moved forward. Then the invoice landed: nearly four times the estimate I'd been given for the work. There was no way I'd ever be able to privately prosecute anything without losing my home.

It was while I was in this muddled state that Kate casually suggested filing a new police report on just the video and letting the criminal justice system have another try. So, when I was let down, yet again, and didn't feel like I had the energy to fight for a rape prosecution anymore – that I just couldn't keep running into the same wall over and over again and hope to get a semblance of a life back – Kate's clever idea was still in the back of my mind. With the profile I'd built up in the press as a public rape victim, surely the police and the prosecutors would take my case seriously if they had another chance.

I could not have been more wrong.

I sat, crumpled, in a fluorescent mustard-coloured waiting-room armchair, with an envelope in my lap and the letter on top of it. Words side up, it had started to catch my tears and I watched as a splash grew into a larger stain on the page.

It was April of 2019, nearly four years after I'd been raped, and I was in the window-filled lobby of the Ministry of Justice. People streamed past as I wept. The letter was from the CPS, announcing that, regardless of the evidence, regardless of the fact that John had admitted to every aspect of the crime of voyeurism, and even though the government believed that the intention of the Sexual Offences Act of 2003 that codified voyeurism as a crime covered exactly the sort of offence John had admitted to, the prosecutors did not believe that a crime had been committed. There would be no justice.

It had been a disaster from the moment I filed the police report. Even more of a disaster than I thought possible. From the beginning, I made it clear that this had nothing to do with the rape. However, when the police took more than two months to locate the evidence from the first investigation, and then took ages to review it – they made it clear that they were refusing to treat the two crimes separately.

The police assigned to the investigation refused to interview me and insisted that my previous statement from May 2015 would be sufficient. When I pointed out that at that time I had no idea the video even existed so that statement clearly couldn't be used, I was ignored. When I reminded the police that under the Victims' Code I had a right to submit a Victim Personal Statement, I was told that I would be asked for one when they wanted one: they never did ask for it. The case file went to the CPS without any sort of statement from me regarding the video. I'd filed the police report in July 2018, and it was just days before Christmas when the CPS made their initial decision to not prosecute John for voyeurism.

Their decision was shocking. They said that as I couldn't remember the events of that evening, then I couldn't prove I didn't consent to John taking the video. Given that John had admitted in his police interview that he knew he didn't have my permission to take the video, it became clear very quickly that the police and the CPS hadn't even done the bare minimum of work on this. They were only interested in discrediting me, not in my attacker's confession.

Then came the next affront. They continued to insist that even if it could be proved that my attacker didn't have my consent to take the video, that it was not illegal to take a photo or a video of someone naked without their permission if you were in the same room as them. Anyone who was allowed to see you naked was also allowed to take an intimate image of you and keep it forever, even if you were standing in the frame saying, "You do not have my permission to take this video." Consent to sex, or consent to being seen, was consent to having your image owned and used by someone else indefinitely. I immediately asked the CPS to review their decision.

A few nights later, on New Year's Eve, my daughter and I sat on the couch at my mother's house in the United States and watched the ball drop over New York City on television. 2019 began like so many previous years, with me hoping, trying, pushing, needing something to happen, for there to be some sort of resolution. For something to go my way, just the once. Instead, it was like every year since 2015.

The CPS refused my first appeal to take my case forward.[63] By my last appeal, they had finally got

---

63 Just under 15% of Victim Right to Review appeals on sex offences result in the CPS changing its original decision. https://www.cps.gov.uk/underlying-data/victims-right-review-data-2019-2020

their facts right. But to the end, they insisted that the law did not cover what had happened to me; one did not have a reasonable expectation of privacy while in an intimate situation. And so, I sat in that mustard armchair in the waiting area in the Ministry of Justice and prepared to give up. Or to fight. And I cried even more because I didn't know which.

On October 16, 2018, police entered Tony Richards' home in Caerau, Wales, looking for indecent images of children that Richards had downloaded from the internet.[64] And they found them, including videos of children as young as one being abused. But amongst these horrible videos, they also found two videos they weren't expecting: Richards having sex with adult women, and it was clear the women didn't know they were being filmed. Richards was arrested and eventually charged, not just for possession of the indecent images of children, but for voyeurism on the basis of the secret sex videos. According to newspaper reports, when told he was being charged

---

64   https://www.walesonline.co.uk/news/wales-news/sex-work-cardiff-prostitute-prostitution-16691336

with voyeurism, he asked quite bluntly, "What's voyeurism?"

After the CPS told me that what had happened to me wasn't illegal, I asked an acquaintance to run a survey for me. I wanted to understand if my thoughts about voyeurism were in line with other people's. The results were stark. In December 2017,[65] 76% of people in the UK believed that it was already illegal to video someone naked without their permission. When told it wasn't already illegal, 81% wanted it made illegal immediately.

The Richards case, as I found out much later, had been running in parallel to my voyeurism case almost from the beginning. The police didn't start really looking at my complaint of voyeurism against John until September or October 2018. When they sent the file to the CPS that autumn, Tony Richards had likely already been charged with voyeurism or was just about to be. Certainly by the time the CPS confirmed just before Christmas that they weren't going to prosecute John – in part because it was not illegal to video someone naked without their consent

---

65   Private polling, December 2017, nat. rep. sample online from Opinium.

if you were in the same room – they'd already set the wheels in motion by charging Richards with exactly that crime, and setting a trial date for July 2019.

I sat at the bar of the Holborn Dining Room on the Thursday before Easter 2019. It was a couple of weeks after the CPS had given me their decision on my final appeal to not prosecute John for voyeurism. I'd cried for days. I'd written an update to my supporters letting them know I was considering my options, but that realistically, it might be the end of the road.

I had exactly one move left, and it was high risk. I could bring a judicial review against the CPS and essentially ask a judge to force them to read the law the way the government said they intended it to be read. There were no guarantees, however, that a court would grant permission for a judicial review, and even fewer guarantees that I would win. If I didn't win, I would be personally liable for the costs: not just the cost of bringing the judicial review, but the CPS's costs in fighting it.

My friend Gavin was sitting next to me on a high red barstool as a waiter in a tartan uniform poured our drinks behind the bar.

Chapter Five

"I don't think you should do it," he said. "You could lose your house."

"I know."

"I think it could also be really draining and difficult for you emotionally. You've been doing so well."

He had a point. I'd been getting a few small freelance jobs, including the one I'd met Gavin on, and was hoping that more projects were on their way. It felt like I might be on my way back to at least something resembling a normal life. And if I went forward with the judicial review, I would be putting that at risk with every legal hurdle that would bring me low, every press interview that would steal my energy, all of it. But I was having an impossible time imagining leaving this as it was.

"If I don't do the judicial review, then I won't be able to change the law," I reminded him. "I feel like I can't leave it like this. We can't live in a country where it is legal for someone to video someone else naked without their permission like this, it's insane."

In convincing him, I had nearly convinced myself.

Six weeks later, with time running out for the judicial review, I sat down with Kate Ellis and her boss, Harriet Wistrich, the founder of the Centre for Women's Justice. Whichever way you looked at it, it was a risk, but after talking through a crowd-funding strategy, it felt like a manageable risk. With just days to go – and while unbeknownst to us Tony Richards was waiting for his trial to start the following month – we began raising money, and the Centre for Women's Justice team began the legal process for me to bring a judicial review against the CPS.

Although we still didn't know about Tony Richards, a journalist had unearthed another voyeurism case that the CPS had already prosecuted. In 2017, they'd successfully prosecuted former police officer Jayson Lobo for voyeurism, on the basis of a trove of videos of himself having sex with women, who were clearly being filmed without their permission.[66] We included this case in our letter to the CPS, informing them that we'd be bringing a judicial review imminently unless they changed their point of view.

At the end of June 2019, the CPS made it clear in a letter to my legal team that they were going to fight tooth and nail to keep me from seeing any sort of justice served. They insisted, again, that

---

66   https://www.bbc.co.uk/news/uk-england-lancashire-41701538

the law was on their side, despite the fact they had previously successfully prosecuted someone else for this crime; despite the fact they were preparing for Tony Richards' trial in just three weeks' time.

On August 8, 2019, a Twitter contact sent me a link to a story about Tony Richards.[67] I sent it on to my lawyers, who referenced it along with the other case we'd found in letters to the CPS after that.

But it didn't change anything.

I was, under no circumstances, a worthy-enough victim for the CPS. It was, however, so important for them to not back down that they spent countless hours and a huge amount of taxpayers' money fighting common sense and their own precedent. From that first letter in June 2019 to when the court granted permission for me to bring the judicial review, we asked the CPS time and time again to drop their resistance. They refused. Our trial was set for February 6, 2020. I was finally going to have my day in court, except instead of John being the defendant, it was the CPS who would, at least metaphorically, be in the dock.

---

67   https://www.mirror.co.uk/news/uk-news/pervert-secretly-filmed-sex-prostitutes-18858871

* * *

Two weeks before we were due in the Royal Courts of Justice, I was sitting on the blue couch in my living room with my feet up on the old wooden travelling trunk that I use as a coffee table when my phone rang.

"I just wanted to give you a heads-up," said Kate over the phone, with an obvious note of concern in her voice. "We went to drop off our skeleton legal argument at the court today and were told that the hearing had been adjourned."

"I don't understand, what does that mean?" I asked.

"We're trying to get to the bottom of it, but it seems that there is another voyeurism case happening next week, so the week before ours. This other one is in the Criminal Court of Appeal, and that's a higher court. The CPS is arguing that our case should be thrown out because the point of law that our case concerns is the same as this other one – whether or not it's legally voyeurism to video someone naked if you're in the same room."

"The CPS is arguing what?"

"In this other case, the CPS is saying that it is illegal to video someone naked even if they are in the same room. They're saying it's voyeurism. But what's most insane is that they are trying to have our case adjourned – so thrown out – and are still refusing to drop their resistance to your judicial review."

The world started to tunnel to a point on the far wall, as it occurred to me that the CPS was literally involved in two separate cases that would be heard in the same building just a week apart. They were literally involved in two separate cases in which they were arguing exactly opposite points of law. In the Tony Richards case, it was illegal. In my case? It wasn't. And even though they'd had this pointed out to them, they still refused to consider charging John.

My mind was reeling. That small measure of control that I'd fought so hard for, the slim possibility of hope and justice that had just been within grabbing distance, suddenly evaporated.

Kate went on. "We're asking the court to let us participate in the other hearing, to essentially formally intervene and share our legal argument. All is not lost yet, but I just wanted to warn you that the hearing might not be happening on the 6th."

The next week, in his white wig and black robes, my barrister, Jude Bunting, stood up in the Criminal Appeal Court and began laying out our case. He stood next to the CPS barristers, referencing the argument they'd just presented – and improving it for them. Because suddenly, we were all fighting on the same side. We were all saying that in the Tony Richards case, it was clearly illegal to video someone naked without their consent, even if you were in the same room.

The CPS had refused my team's help in the Richards case, and yet the courts imposed us on them. In an unprecedented move I, as an individual, was allowed to formally intervene in a Criminal Appeals Court case to which I had no actual connection. Yet, even though we were going to court with them, in support of their case, the CPS still refused to drop their resistance to my judicial review or consider charging my attacker; on principle, they said. They wanted to wait and see what happened in this criminal appeal.

After all three sets of barristers – the CPS, mine and the defence – made their cases, the judges retired to prepare their judgement. Upon returning, Lord Justice Fulford took his place in the middle of the panel of three judges and began to read out their decision. The wood-panelled courtroom was silent, apart from the sounds of typing – and Lord Justice Fulford's words.

He began by summarising the details of the Richards case thus far and the various legal arguments made. And then, with one sentence, he changed my life.

"The presence of the appellant as one of the participants in the intercourse does not lessen the reasonable expectation of privacy in this sense," he said of Tony Richards and the women he'd had sex with in the videos. "Namely that what occurred would not be available for later viewing, even if only by the appellant." In the court's view, Tony Richards was guilty of voyeurism. The law, as written and when properly applied, already protected someone from being filmed by someone in the same room as them, even in an intimate setting. There were no longer two ways of interpreting the law. We had won. Along with the CPS.

It took a couple of hours for the CPS to agree to drop their resistance to my judicial review and agree to reconsider their decision not to prosecute John for voyeurism. When Kate rang me with the news, I was sitting in a pub with one of my oldest friends, Victor, whom I'd been close to since I was five years old. When Kate started to explain the news to me, I yelled, burst out crying and raised my arms in victory.

It took a further three and a half months for the CPS to complete their review of the voyeurism case against John. In May 2020, just over five years after the incident – just over two years after Kate Ellis suggested I submit a new crime report based on the video alone – John was finally charged with a sex offence: voyeurism.

The first hearing was set for August 7, and he gave every indication that he intended to plead guilty.

Chapter Six

John leaned awkwardly with his elbows against the edge of the dock – it was too low for him, really, so he looked uncomfortable and out of place. Dressed in a rumpled blue linen shirt, casual trousers and worn trainers, he had arrived at the Thames Magistrates' Court on the sweltering morning of August 7 with a rucksack slung over his shoulder. It was one of the hottest days of 2020 and the courthouse itself seemed to be sweating under the weight of the midsummer sun. The gallery was relatively packed with journalists, as well as my friend Gavin and my solicitor, Kate Ellis.

Though he'd known about the court date for three months, John arrived with no solicitor, or even friends or family. As the court scrambled to find a duty solicitor to advise him for the hearing, he negotiated the warren of courthouse passages and encountered the press for the first time.

"How are you going to plead?" one reporter asked him as he waited outside the courtroom.

"I don't know. Guilty I guess, so long as this isn't about that rape thing."

When he stood before District Judge Louisa Ciecióra in the dock a few hours later, she asked him the same question. John continued to lean on the edge of the dock and made no move to answer.

The judge asked again, "How do you plead on the charge of voyeurism?"

John looked up at her and said, "Hold on, I need to think about it for a moment."

He paused again and the courtroom waited. The judge regarded him sharply and the prosecutor turned to stare. For a moment, it seemed as though he would upset the script. Finally, he said the word:

"Guilty."

He was bailed on condition of not contacting me until his sentencing the following month.

When John was arrested on suspicion of rape, he told the police that he was the least likely rapist ever. However, he also told the police that night that he thought I might be mentally ill and that he'd asked me if I was on drugs because I was so obviously heavily intoxicated. Either of those two observations made it highly unlikely he could reasonably believe I was capable of giving consent for sex.

Add to that the inescapable and undisputed fact that he was entirely sober at the time, and it becomes very hard to see how John's actions did not constitute rape. However, although he disputed that he was guilty of that accusation, he freely admitted in his police interview that he took the naked video of me without my permission and he also said he masturbated next to me and ejaculated onto my thigh. He was willing to admit to other sex offences, but not rape – and it appears that that continues to be his position. Regardless of the mounting wall of evidence to the contrary, including from his own statement, John does not see his behaviour as rape.

John is not unique on this front.

In a 2014 study,[68] male students at an American university were asked to participate in a survey. In one question, they were asked to consider that if there were no consequences, would they force someone to have "sex against their will". In another question, again if there were no consequences, they were asked if they would "rape" someone. Forcing someone to have sex against their will is the literal definition of rape – but the students' reactions showed that there is a huge disconnect between the action of rape and the word. While only 14% of participants said they'd rape someone in this hypothetical situation, 32% of the participants said they'd force someone to have sex against their will.[69]

This idea that "rape" and "non-consensual sex" are seen as two different things is repeatedly confirmed in academic study after academic study. Indeed, in just one study of convicted rapists, researchers found that 28% of them would admit to every detail of their crimes, but would not consider

---

68   https://www.researchgate.net/publication/291567285_ Denying_Rape_but_Endorsing_Forceful_Intercourse_ Exploring_Differences_Among_Responders
69   *ibid.*

their behaviour to be "rape".[70] In other words, even those convicted of rape who admit the detail of what they've done, still consider the specific crime of "rape" to be so heinous and incomprehensible that they can't accept they've committed it.

It's obvious this disconnect is inextricably interlinked to our societal belief in rape myths. We blame the victim because the rapist blames the victim, and the rapist blames the victim because we blame the victim. Against this backdrop, it's easy for a rapist to deny what he has done and downplay his behaviour by saying it wasn't rape, or that it wasn't non-consensual sex. Or, regardless of that, she wanted it. Or, as we saw in Chapter Two, she flirted and therefore owed the man sex.[71] There are innumerable reasons and ways for a rapist to tell himself and others in his life that he hasn't committed rape, that he's not that type of man, that the victim shared at least part, if not all, of the blame.

---

70   *ibid.*

71   https://www.endviolenceagainstwomen.org.uk/wp-content/uploads/Data-tables-for-Attitudes-to-Sexual-Consent-research-report.pdf

Therefore, many of these people don't see what they've done as wrong because they don't see their actions as fitting the category of rape. We should not then be surprised when they come across as very believable when they say they're innocent. However, believing you haven't committed rape when you actually have is not a legal defence. Even if a man feels entitled to have sex with someone who hasn't given their consent, even if he believes it doesn't count as rape because she flirted or led him on or any other reason he has in mind, it still is. And it can, and should, be prosecuted.

When other crimes are committed, we don't tend to blame the victim or ask what they did to deserve it, or believe the perpetrator when they say it wasn't really a crime. In March 2017, Tracey Ullman did a skit for BBC One, squarely spinning victim-blaming on its head: a well-dressed man is in a police station giving his statement after being mugged.[72] Every sort of question that a rape victim is eventually asked comes up, one after the other.

---

72   https://www.dailymail.co.uk/news/article-4313076/Tracey-Ullman-sexual-assault-sketch-divides-internet.html

"Is this what you were wearing when it happened?" asks the female police officer. He's then asked if he'd perhaps led the mugger on by wearing a nice suit and not making it clear that he didn't want to hand over his phone. He's told that drinking alcohol might have resulted in the mugger getting mixed signals from him on whether he wanted to be mugged or not. And while the entire exercise is more than a bit silly, the point is valid. No one wants to be mugged, just as no one wants to be raped. If we then think "but it's different because people like to have sex," a similar argument could be made about people liking to give and receive gifts. We don't ask a mugging victim to prove that the crime happened, and we don't doubt their account. Even more so, we don't doubt whether or not they wanted to be mugged.

When my laptop bag was stolen in 2012,[73] I was in a bar drinking. But that had no bearing on any of the questions the police asked me. At no point was it implied that these things happen, or that perhaps I should just be more careful with my belongings. The police did not say that if I didn't report it, no one would find out. No one asked if the crime had

---

73   See Chapter Three.

really happened. No one judged the loss of my bag based on the amount of alcohol I'd consumed or what I was wearing. The police immediately conducted their investigation and caught the culprits. My worthiness as a victim was never part of their calculation. I didn't need to be righteous, perfect or even vaguely likeable. I was believed and they did their jobs.

As we explored earlier, rapists have no type. There is nothing a victim can do that causes their rape, and no commonality other than that most rape victims are female and many are between 18–65 years old. While a rapist might want to blame the victim, the stark reality is that the only cause of rape is rapists. But if it isn't the victim's fault, why do rapists rape?

I had a friend who confessed to me not long after I was raped that when he went out on dates, he'd always come back from the bar with a large glass of wine or a double gin if the woman he was with asked for a small glass of wine or a single in her gin and tonic. If he was caught out, he'd feign that he hadn't heard correctly or had forgotten the order. He, in a gentlemanly way, with his affable demeanour, would buy every round, always bringing back a larger drink than ordered. He said to me that, of course, he did this to soften his dates up. It would increase his chances of taking one home. He saw nothing wrong with it.[74]

Where is the line intellectually between what this person did and someone putting a small amount of a date-rape drug like GHB into a drink to "soften" someone up, as I suspect happened to me? Think about it another way: GHB is occasionally used recreationally by people, diabetics for example, who can't or don't drink alcohol, because in small amounts it can mimic the effects of alcohol. For someone who doesn't drink alcohol, it could very easily just be a normal part of socialising in a pub. So is there any difference between that person spiking a drink with GHB, and my former friend purposely buying drinks with more alcohol in them than their date wanted? It is different − one involves an illegal substance that the date has not consented to having − but the motivation behind both is very similar. What then is the difference if, in each instance, the man was not drinking or using drugs himself, just

---

74   It is likely not surprising, but we are no longer friends.

providing them, either completely surreptitiously, or in larger amounts than expected or wanted?

It is, frankly, uncomfortable to think about either scenario. Because really, some of this is very normal Friday-night behaviour for a lot of quite normal people.

What rapists often have in common is that straying over a fuzzy line, first slowly, then existing in that grey area, and then going over so far to the other side that they can't see the line anymore. It is the proverbial boiling of a frog: by the time a rapist is raping, a lot of the behaviour that leads to that moment may very well have become normalised for them. It's often one small step, not a giant leap.

This line-crossing tends to start young, in secondary school or early on in university, and often involves someone the budding rapist knows.[75] A few longitudinal studies have seen this behaviour as a burst of sexual aggression in younger men, largely opportunistic and transitory,[76] which in many cases

75   "What Experts Know About Men Who Rape" https://www. nytimes.com/2017/10/30/health/men-rape-sexual-assault.html

76   https://corpus.ulaval.ca/jspui/bitstream/20.500.11794/1 1108/1/Lussier%26Cale_2016_depotUL.pdf

fades away. The assumption is that they rape a few times and are then likely to stop. However, this isn't always the case. Again, as discussed earlier, the majority of rapists who aren't caught go on to do it again, raping on average 5.8 times over the course of their lives,[77] and while some of this may be early in their lives, it won't all be.[78]

But the actual reasons that these men rape involve a constellation of confusing, overlapping and often even contradictory factors. Of course, given that even men who have been jailed for rape and have admitted to the details of their crimes still don't agree they've actually committed rape, there are difficulties in really unpicking what is real and what isn't. Over the last 50 or more years of academic study in this area, there have been numerous discussions on what causes rape: mental illness; the desire to impose the will of patriarchy;

---

77 "Repeat rape and multiple offending among undetected rapists" https://www.documentcloud.org/documents/1699822-2002-lisak-repeatrapeinundetectedrapists.html

78 Project Bluestone in Avon & Somerset found that in a review of sex offence files over three years, nearly a quarter of named suspects had been named in another sex offence case. About 60% were known to the police for one reason or other.

the nature of evolution, and more. Based on this, we can start to peel back the layers and at least look at some of the factors that underpin this behaviour.

An in-depth review of previous academic literature showed that what rapists really have in common is that they want sexual gratification with someone who does not at that time want to have sex with them,[79] someone who has not or cannot give consent. This may seem basic, but has actually been hotly debated over the years. Otherwise, the research has found no "single master-cause" of rape.[80] Instead, a network of causes, factors and goals contribute to any one rapist's actions.[81]

Essentially, there is no single answer.

Perhaps an important starting point for understanding this is that most men who commit rape aren't sexually aroused by it; a meta-review of studies has shown that only a minority of convicted sex offenders find such situations innately arousing.[82]

---

79   https://www.jstor.org/stable/23074037
80   *ibid.*
81   *ibid.*
82   https://corpus.ulaval.ca/jspui/bitstream/20.500.11794/11108/1/Lussier%26Cale_2016_depotUL.pdf

They don't rape because it's something they fanta-sise about. They rape because they can.

There is then a dichotomy between those who will steal anything and those who will only steal sex. The generalist criminal versus the specialist rapist. In the first group, there are general "criminality" factors that can usually be identified, such as poor self-control, substance use and abuse and the influ-ence of antisocial attitudes and peers.[83] Some of these broad and common criminality factors also express themselves in the specialist group, in particular that rapists, by and large, regardless of their criminal careers or lack of them, aren't inhibited by the fact that their "desired" woman doesn't want to or is unable to consent to have sex with them.

There are hundreds of other factors that academ-ics have considered, from adverse events in childhood to educational attainment, from high sex drive and hyperarousal around women to secret homosexual tendencies, from having too little or too much power over their lives. They vary in importance and valid-ity across different groups and across different time periods, but current research points to connections

83   *ibid.*

with "public attitudes towards victims, the status of women, sex roles, and the likelihood of punishment"[84] as key to understanding rapists, and also how to prevent them from raping in the first place.

In autumn 2020, the private messages of a group of about 60 young men, many of whom were about to begin their first year at Durham University, were posted on a public forum. Their messages were largely innocuous "lad banter" that could be written off as the blustering of boys pretending to be men. But in amongst the bad taste and general posing was the suggestion of a contest to see who could sleep with the poorest female student, and an open discussion normalising the idea of spiking a woman's drink in order to have sex with her.[85] The language was vile, and the fact that anyone would be comfortable enough with those ideas to actually write them down made it even worse.

I sent a link to the article to my friend, Gavin, who is the father of a university-age daughter.

---

84   https://www.jstor.org/stable/23074037
85   https://www.dailymail.co.uk/news/article-8713083/
Posh-lads-Durham-University-planned-competition-sex-poorest-girl-campus.html

"That actually is a bit of a punch in the gut," he wrote back. As we chatted more about it, the point he kept coming back to was that a number of the participants in the group seemed to be expressing real venom towards women in general. These young men seemed to really hate the female students they'd be studying with, apparently simply because they were female, but even more so because they were the perceived gatekeepers to having sex. We discussed whether attitudes towards women were getting worse, as Gavin was shocked not only by the language and ideas, but more so at how much angrier and more extreme they seemed, compared to the laddish banter he'd experienced in locker rooms while in his 20s.[86]

"What's needed is (a) for there to be perceived consequences, and (b) for young guys not even to think this is a remotely acceptable way to talk. This should be as socially unacceptable as racism or homophobia," he wrote to me later that afternoon.

---

86 There needs to be further research and serious discussion on this, as there is obviously a burgeoning body of literature about whether or not easy access to extreme pornography is dehumanising women – and sex – for young men.

"It says so much about some young men and how much their attitudes need to change."

It was the lack of empathy for women – as women and, frankly, just as human beings – that made these participants in the Durham group chat similar to both generalist criminal rapists and specialist rapists.[87] Lack of empathy for women is another factor that both groups have in common, and while it could be considered a part of the perceived "status of women" that came out in the meta-review of literature, I think it's even more important in understanding how some men cross the line between slightly suspect behaviour and rape.

How someone thinks about the role of women in society is almost impersonal. You're asking how someone feels about a hypothetical. An abstract. When a young man is in a bar, faced with a young woman he'd like to have sex with, if he doesn't recognise her as an individual, as a person, as a human being, with her own needs, wants and feelings, if he can't have empathy for her – or doesn't want to have empathy for her at that moment – it's much easier to

---

87   https://corpus.ulaval.ca/jspui/bitstream/20.500.11794/11108/1/Lussier%26Cale_2016_depotUL.pdf

understand how he can then convince himself that having sex with her without her consent isn't rape.

No one can say for certain if any of the young men in that group chat would ever have acted upon what they were discussing, but those participating in the conversation were demonstrating in the real world some of the attributes which had already been discovered in the academic world: no consequences for rape; peers who think rape is acceptable; victim-blaming; lack of empathy for women; and wanting to have sex with someone regardless of whether or not they consent – all factors that can contribute to young men crossing that line and becoming rapists.

If we want to prevent this happening, the most important of the plausible causes of rape to address are social factors, such as low empathy, rape myths and the likely lack of punishment, but also the lesser sex offences that might precede a first rape.[88] If that's the case, then, unfortunately, we're going in the wrong direction as a society. And in doing that, we are failing young men. If 32% of men would force someone to have sex with them against their will if there were no consequences, in a country where

---

88   https://www.jstor.org/stable/23074037

only 1.3% of reported rapes are prosecuted and conversations about raping classmates and spiking their drinks with drugs can be seen as acceptable, how can we not expect the actual number of rapes to start going up in the future?[89]

On the day of John's first hearing, while Gavin and Kate sat in the courtroom gallery watching it unfold in real time, I was sitting in a scruffy side room of the courthouse. It was the CPS office in the court, as there was no witness or victim waiting area. There was nowhere else for me to sit where I could be sure not to run into John or members of his family or friends, had he brought any along. Paint was missing from the walls where posters had once been. One of the desk chairs was broken, with packing tape inelegantly applied to keep anyone from sitting on it. Someone had brought me a glass of water while we waited.

I had been asked to attend the hearing to potentially read out my Victim Personal Statement in

---

89   While rape reports have been going up in the last few years, as best we can tell, the actual number of rapes has stayed relatively level.

court ahead of sentencing,[90] assuming John pleaded guilty. Considering he had admitted every aspect of the crime of voyeurism in his police statement, he couldn't realistically plead any other way.

It had been a rough couple of weeks for me. I had originally intended to read out a very short, two-paragraph statement glossing over what John had done to me and simply saying that it had had a profound impact on me. I was trying to trust the system now that my case was finally going to be heard in court. When I found out that the prosecutors were planning on holding the hearing and sentencing at the same time, it meant they weren't seeking any sort of medium or high-level punishment. Even a community order would have required a pre-sentencing report and two court hearings: the first, to declare guilt and a second down the line for sentencing.

I was trying to be at peace with it. I had for all intents and purposes changed the law on voyeurism

---

90   After John was charged in May 2020, the police officer who refused to take my statement on the video was instructed by the CPS to obtain a formal statement. I gave it at a police station in June, more than five years after the video was taken. I was finally allowed to write my Victim Personal Statement after that.

and made what happened to me irrefutably illegal. I'd already been contacted by another victim of voyeurism; the police had taken her case seriously when she reported it and had even explained that my case had made it clear that it was illegal to video someone without their permission in an intimate setting. That was the big win. John was going to get a slap on the wrist and I was going to have to be okay with it. I'd been reading Martha Nussbaum's *Anger and Forgiveness*, in which she explains why she thinks that emotionally charged victim statements do no good, either for the victim or for the justice system. I was resigned to the small measure of justice I was going to get after this five-year battle. I was actively embracing the big win on clarifying the law while letting go of my own case.

But, in late July, I was scrolling through replies to a tweet I'd posted and discovered that just three weeks before the hearing was due to take place, John had publicly tweeted at me. It was the culmination of years of minor harassment from him. Just after I was raped, he'd popped up on my Facebook page as "someone you may know", possibly because he was repeatedly looking at my profile. But there was no way to tell. I reported it to the police, who did nothing. At least it gave me the opportunity to block him.

When I was crowdfunding in October 2017, someone went to the effort of paying in cash for a preloaded debit card which they then used to donate £5, in an entirely untraceable way, to my campaign. Attached to the donation was a horrible trolling message. Their previous attempts at posting similar messages had been deleted by the site administrators before being posted. But the system wasn't set up to protect against someone being so full of anger or hate that they were prepared to pay to post an upsetting message; whoever had posted it had found a way round the system. There were weird details included in the message and it immediately made me feel very uneasy, as it seemed like only John or someone he knew would have known about them. I also reported that to the police, who again did nothing.

The most concerning incident had been in June 2019, when John sent me a series of strange messages on Twitter asking me to meet him in person. He'd originally said that if I didn't reply, he wouldn't contact me again. When he did, Kate suggested I report it to the police. The police apparently had an informal chat with him and told him not to contact me anymore, especially through Twitter. When John was finally charged with voyeurism in May 2020, the police officer who informed him of the charge pointed out that he shouldn't contact anyone involved with the case, as it could be seen as witness intimidation. They meant me.

When John tweeted at me, as irrational as it sounds, it caused my first sustained PTSD episode in a couple of years. I spent two weeks afraid to leave my house with my daughter for fear he'd be waiting for us outside.

When I reported it to the police, they took days to respond. They refused to treat it as witness intimidation until it was passed to another station, who escalated the case to some higher-ups, who were horrified it had been treated as anything other than a suspected sex offender trying to intimidate the only witness in his case. John was arrested, but within a few hours the CPS decided there wasn't enough evidence to prove it was witness intimidation, even though he'd been told that contacting me could be considered exactly that. He was released. I was terrified. If he could do something so brazen

– something that he'd been specifically told not to do – and, in doing it anyway, received no punishment, I began to fear for my safety, both physically and emotionally.

I asked for a restraining order and rewrote my Victim Personal Statement to include everything that had happened on May 10, 2015, as I knew from the evidence and John's statement. I didn't say that I was raped, or even that I couldn't have consented to sex. Instead, I wrote about the CCTV footage of me falling over in the hallway of the hotel and how John was sober. I wrote about how he told the police he thought I was mentally ill or on drugs. I wrote about his ejaculating onto my thigh. And I wrote about the impact on me of finding out about the video. I wrote about having PTSD and nearly losing my life. I wrote that he was a sex offender, a deviant and someone who would go on to do it again. I wrote it all down – carefully, to ensure I wasn't colouring any of the facts – and resubmitted it. I no longer trusted the system to even get the undisputed evidence right. And after all of the fighting to get this case finally heard in a courtroom, the disdain I felt towards me from the police and the

CPS and the panic and fear that John caused me, felt overwhelming.

At 6:38pm, the night before the first hearing, I was sitting on my dark grey sofa under the stairs in my living room. It was after suppertime and in that nice bit of golden time my daughter and I have together between supper and when she goes upstairs to read in the hour before bed. I was nearly ready for court, but was planning on reviewing my statement a few times to be ready to say it aloud, in front of the courtroom. My phone buzzed with an email from the police officer who'd been my liaison ahead of the court date, quite blithely informing me that the prosecutors had decided that my statement couldn't be read out in full the way I'd written it. The digital copy that was attached for me to read out instead had been more than half redacted. I replied saying it wasn't acceptable and that I needed someone to contact me straight away. After my daughter went up to bed, I did the only thing I could, I cried. No one from the police or the CPS contacted me. No one from Victim Support did either.

The next morning, I arrived at the court with Gavin and met Kate there. Considering my PTSD symptoms and the way I felt that the police weren't inclined to keep me safe, I was also accompanied by Paul, a professional bodyguard who was donating his time to help me. I was angry and distrustful and very upset about the situation. Paul led us into a quiet corner of the courthouse to wait. Sitting on three plastic chairs against the wall of the bail office, I spoke to Kate and Gavin.

"What if I refuse to read out the redacted version? Or, what if I just say that he raped me rather than carefully presenting the evidence?"

I couldn't believe that I'd fought so far for so little justice and wouldn't be able to say anything real about what had happened to me that night five years earlier.

When the police officer came down to get our little group, I said that I needed to speak with the CPS immediately about the statement. But then it became clear that the whole world had seemingly shifted overnight. We were no longer there for a minor voyeurism case. The police and CPS no longer expected the entire case to be taken care of in one swift hearing. The outcome would no longer just be a small fine.

The CPS was presenting evidence for a case that potentially met the threshold for a custodial sentence.

I wouldn't be reading my statement out at all that day, and I didn't need to be at court for the hearing anymore. We'd have weeks to agree a new version because, if John pleaded guilty as expected, he'd be bailed until sentencing so the judge could make sure that a pre-sentencing report was compiled.

I sat, while Paul stood, in the CPS office at the side of the Thames Magistrates' Court with Gavin and Kate, watching the hearing in the courtroom. Kate took detailed notes of what the prosecutor was saying. All of a sudden, someone somewhere had realised – after five years – that perhaps this case mattered. That John had nearly broken me. That he had taken advantage of someone vulnerable. That he was a sex offender who would do it again if not stopped. I suspect that someone might have been Varinder Hayre, the prosecutor.

Twenty-one minutes into the hearing, Gavin texted me: "He has pleaded guilty".

Finally, I was vindicated. A few minutes later, Gavin texted again: "And the prosecutor is

reading out everything. Like literally everything"
from my original police statement from May 2015
about what happened that night.

If, in the last 30 years or so, it has been
assumed that about 6% of men are rapists,[91] we
need to remember that almost all of them are
men who strayed across a line. For every 100
men, quite possibly not even one of them will
ever rape a stranger. Five to six of them will,
however, rape someone they know. From John's
perspective, his experience with me was perhaps
something like a date gone wrong – from mine it
was stranger rape.

Everything we say about rape prevention is
wrong: women don't need a rape whistle or need to
walk home at night with their keys between their
fingers or go out in groups to protect each other.
Rape prevention lands squarely on the 6% of men
who rape, the people around them and a criminal
justice system that doesn't prosecute them.

The only cause of rape is rapists, but society has
a role to play in teaching young men the difference

91   Some studies put this as high as 25%, but I tend to think
the truth is probably closer to this lower number.

between right and wrong. When there is little chance of negative consequences for rapists, whether judicially or even in their own social circles and in their lives in general, straying across that line is easier. In addition, when we default to blaming a victim for what she was wearing, or drinking, or for being out on her own, or having someone over to her home, or even just for flirting and so on, we release rapists from blame for their actions. We also make it easier for the people around those rapists to believe that they've been falsely accused.

To tackle rape as an issue, we need to change the conversation.

Chapter Seven

From the moment my attacker pleaded guilty on that hot August day more than five years after I'd woken up next to him in the hotel bed, everything changed. I'd clarified the law on voyeurism and finally seen justice in my own case. Along the way, I'd amassed thousands of supporters and well-wishers who hadn't just helped fund my legal battle but cheered me on and picked me up when I fell down. It had been an unbelievable fight to get to that point – I'd learned so much, and I now felt I had so much more to give back.

But one thing was clear: I no longer had to fight my fight. I could now very easily walk away. I could choose not to attend the sentencing. I could send a written statement to be read out or do nothing. Or, I could attend and say my piece. But it was my choice, and if I wanted, I could finally step away from the fight and do something else.

As I started to think about my next steps, it became more and more obvious to me that I wasn't done. I'd learned so much in my fight, and I felt that I'd somehow managed to reach out to people who didn't necessarily usually engage in conversations about sexual violence. And that even for those who did, I hoped I'd given a little more support to other victims and survivors; it seemed like if I had more to give, I should. I'd contributed to some big conversations. It was time to consider what conversation could come next.

As I walked into Stratford Court at 8:30am on Friday September 4, 2020, photographers were camped outside taking pictures. With Gavin and Paul by my side once again, we made our way into the unfamiliar building, meeting Kate inside. The sentencing had been moved to this courthouse because it had Witness Services, which mostly meant that there was a secure waiting area and a few

volunteer helpers to explain the layout of the courtroom and tell witnesses when it was time to go to the
hearing. The secure waiting area was light and airy
with couches, chairs and big windows. For a while
we were the only ones in the room. It couldn't have
been more different from my previous experience at
court, where all we had was a perch in the CPS's
office with its peeling paint and broken furniture.

Again there was a long wait, as hearings in most
courts don't have set times, they are just called for
the day. The witnesses, victims, various lawyers and
supporters as well as the suspects sit expectantly. I
was lucky that the judge, the same one as for the
first hearing, wanted to get the hearing done early.
Despite that we still had to wait.

The night before the sentencing had been a
rough one for me. I went back and forth and considered not reading my Victim Personal Statement as
I'd planned. I was worried that I was in too fragile
a state and that the stress was going to be too much
for me. I'd done a two-and-a-half-hour-long filmed
interview with the BBC that day and been caught
in a rainstorm on the way home. I never exactly
loved doing media, but I often felt that it was the

best way for me to explain not just my story, but how my experience was far from unique. How rape is so deeply prevalent and how we need, as a society, to start recognising the fact that rape victims don't really lie about rape. I felt like looking into a camera was the best way to help people see that rape victims are just normal people, who've had a truly horrible thing happen to them through no fault of their own. Talking about what happened to me, not just the particulars of my case but the way that the system failed me, was important. But it always took a toll.

By the time I got home from the filming, I was cold and shaking and couldn't get warm. It's a fairly usual physical symptom of PTSD for me. It helps me to know that it's likely that I'll have some irrational thoughts and weird stress responses. I chatted with Gavin over text and we ended up on the phone late into the night as he reassured me that if I wanted to, I absolutely was strong enough to read out my Victim Personal Statement in court the next day. But also, that I didn't have to.

In the time between the two hearings, the statement had been chopped and changed quite a lot by the CPS and by the District Judge. Over and over again the same glaring disconnect resurfaced: I wasn't allowed to talk about what were clearly acknowledged facts of the case and the evidence. In particular I wasn't allowed to reference parts of my attacker's actual police statement given under caution that were admissions of other crimes, things like him knowing he didn't have my permission to masturbate onto me while I slept or that he thought before he had sex with me that I might be mentally ill or on drugs, meaning I wasn't allowed to reference some of the evidence of my extreme intoxication. In my original version of the Victim Personal Statement, I'd been careful and didn't directly accuse John of any crimes other than the one he'd admitted to, but the facts – the acknowledged and undisputed facts of the evening I woke up next to John – were said to be too damning and were removed from my statement. This was the main reason for my reluctance to turn up and read it: after five years, I wasn't actually going to say what I wanted to say.

There were three main possibilities for sentencing: a community order, a suspended sentence or a custodial sentence. John would likely have been told to bring a small bag with him to court that day in case he was given a custodial sentence: it would have started immediately. I thought it very unlikely he'd actually get prison time: with a global pandemic raging, prisons were full of Covid cases and John had a health issue that put him at higher risk. An alternative would have been a suspended sentence, meaning he'd be given a custodial sentence but not actually have to serve it in prison as long as he met the court's conditions and stayed out of trouble. Both a custodial sentence and a suspended sentence would also have meant time on the sex offenders register as a matter of course. Either a custodial sentence or a suspended sentence would likely have been for no more than a month or two. A community order would mean not going to prison, but instead could have a variety of requirements attached to it, including a curfew, community service, attending a rehabilitation programme, and so on. If it were under 12 months, John wouldn't land on the sex offenders register.

Two things were important for me: I wanted John on the sex offenders register so that anyone else who encountered him would be able to find out what sort of person he was. I also wanted a restraining order, keeping him from ever contacting me again. I was still unsettled by his Twitter contact and I didn't want him ever to be able to interrupt my life like that again. With these two things in mind, I decided just hours before we headed to court that I would indeed read out my Victim Personal Statement. Even if the statement itself wasn't what I wanted it to be.

I uncreased the folded pieces of paper as Kate, Gavin, Paul and I sat in the waiting room, to review the words I'd be allowed to say. "I do not know John Doe.[92] From my perspective, we have met just once: when I woke up naked in a hotel bed next to him, with a five-hour blank in my memory. Essentially, all I know about him is what I've learned from his statement and other evidence gathered by the police."

Below that followed seven blacked outlines. And then: "However I got into the state I was in,

---

92   As mentioned earlier, in court, for the first and last time, I used my attacker's name publicly. It's not just in public, though. I don't use his name at all, not in writing or in conversation. If he's mentioned at all, it's usually as "my attacker" or "XY". It's not that he has power over me and I'm afraid to use his name, it's the opposite. For me, this is how I make sure he has no power or place in my life. I chose to have him, essentially, not exist.

I was so deeply intoxicated that there is CCTV of me falling backwards in the hallway outside the hotel room while Mr Doe went to open the door." Then three more blacked-out lines. "After having sex with me, Mr Doe masturbated over me while I slept. He ejaculated onto my thigh and the bed. We know he did this because he admitted it to the police." More blacked-out lines. "He then took a video of me naked which he told officers he planned to masturbate to at a later date. As I was asleep, I did not and could not consent to this. Indeed, he told the police that he knew that he didn't have my permission to take the video and that if I'd woken up while he was taking it, that I would likely have been upset. I believe this context is vitally important in understanding the kind of person Mr Doe is, and to understand the true nature of his voyeurism."

It continued: "This voyeuristic, creepy video wasn't taken after sex between two partners. Nor was it a video taken after sex between two people on an equal level of intoxication after getting to know each other over a few drinks. This video was taken following sex that occurred about an hour after he met me." A blacked-out line and a half and then:

"To me it feels like a trophy." I sighed and shut the papers back along their creased edge. What followed was an almost entirely blacked-out page.

As light filtered in through the large windows, proceedings were starting, so Kate gathered her things to go into the courtroom to watch the prosecutor, Varinder Hayre, begin to make her case for sentencing. I wasn't needed yet, so Paul, Gavin and I made small talk during the interminable wait.

As we chatted, another woman was ushered into the Witness Waiting Room and sat in a comfortable chair by the window. She had no one with her supporting her. Because victims of crimes aren't formally viewed as anything other than a witness to what has happened, there isn't a separate way of dealing with the crime victim themselves or someone who just happened to see the crime occur. Should you be violently attacked on a street for no reason, you would be in the witness room, but also so would someone who simply witnessed a violent attack on the street to which they had no connection. Those two people would be treated in largely the same way. That's the way the system works. The prosecution isn't there to fight for justice for a victim, it is there to present the facts in an objective manner on behalf of the Crown. As a result, the victim in a crime can often feel like an easily forgotten cog in the criminal justice machine. Without them nothing works, but they are so often ignored.

One of the volunteer Witness Waiting Room attendants came in and sat down in our little cluster of chairs, pulling out a folder. She was young, likely in her early 20s. She had long hair and perfect make-up. She wasn't dressed as you would expect a professional in a courthouse role to dress: no dark skirt suit or sensible court shoes. She was wearing what appeared to be black leather trousers. I wondered if it was on purpose to help witnesses feel more at ease. As she opened the folder, she found that it was missing the papers she was meant to show me. There should have been a diagram, maybe even some pictures, of the courtroom.

"I can just explain it," she said, with a sigh.

She seemed less annoyed than resigned. As she began to explain the proceedings that I'd be walking into shortly, it became clear that she actually didn't know what I was there for, what sort of hearing it was or if I was a victim or just a bystander.

"Before you give evidence," she said, "you'll have to take an oath, and there's a little book there for you to read the oath from."

"But I'm not giving evidence, so do I still take an oath?" I asked, genuinely wondering. I had no problem taking an oath, it's just that no one had mentioned it previously.

"What do you mean you're not giving evidence?"

"I'm here to read a Victim Personal Statement in a sentencing hearing," I explained.

"Oh! Um, I don't know if you do the oath then. Let me see if I can go find out," she said as she stood and left the room. I don't actually remember her coming back with the answer, but that might be the fault of my memory rather than the attendant.

Eventually, another CPS prosecutor came into the Witness Waiting Room and went over to the woman by the windows. He was glistening with perspiration and his suit jacket hung from his shoulders awkwardly. He appeared to have been running from one case to another, more in reality than metaphorically. He stood by the woman, nearly in the centre of the large waiting room, not far from where we were sitting. He launched into a few explanations and questions for her. It soon became clear that she was also not just a witness but a victim. Her ex-partner had been stalking her and harassing her, and, according to the woman, had even broken into her flat and assaulted her in an effort to get her to drop the case against him. The CPS prosecutor seemed exasperated with the victim.

"This hearing isn't about that," he said, completely missing the point that she was very understandably afraid of her ex-partner and concerned about what he would do next.

And then the victim mentioned that she had a learning disability, and the prosecutor turned visibly red with anger.

"You didn't tell us that," he said, his voice starting to rise.

He started to berate the victim, who had been harassed by her ex-partner as recently as the previous night and who was receiving not even a minimal amount of compassion or concern. Gavin and I were shocked and horrified by his behaviour. We both knew that prosecutors have too many cases, too little time to prep and, often, don't seem to have the empathy to understand that victims are real people. Perhaps it's because they're overworked in such an overstretched system; perhaps it's a lack of imagination; perhaps something else. But, regardless of the cause, few of those prosecuting on behalf of the CPS in my experience, and from other victims I've spoken to, seem to have the capacity to deal with victims, particularly those traumatised by the crimes committed against them.

Even that may be unfair to a certain extent on the CPS. My entire experience with the criminal justice system had shown me that no one seemed to understand that a victim hasn't made a choice to interact with the system; they didn't want to be there; they weren't placing unreasonable demands on anyone; they'd rather not be involved at all. This is true of all crime victims but perhaps even more striking with rape victims. No one chooses to be raped: that is essentially the definition of the crime. A rape victim is someone who has had their choice, control and dignity taken from them. Someone has had sex with them without their consent. There probably isn't a more heinous crime short of murder. But then they enter the system and, instead of being treated as victims, more often than not, they end up feeling like the suspect. Indeed, unlike any other crime I can find in the criminal justice system, we explicitly investigate the rape victim or "complainant" before, or realistically in lieu of, the rape suspect.[93]

This bears repeating: in rape cases across the country, it is only when the victim has been deemed credible that the crime or the suspect is investigated. No other crime is dealt with in the same way.

It cannot then be surprising that 58% of rape victims stop participating in their cases,[94] meaning they either refuse to hand over evidence – as in my case when I refused to hand over my mobile phone for what is now often referred to as a "digital strip search" – or they don't agree to share their medical records, or they drop out along the way so they can seek counselling or simply move on with their lives. Currently, even with only 1.3% of rape cases resulting in charges being brought, there is still at

---

93   This has theoretically changed as of 2021, with all police forces and the CPS committing to training on suspect-focused investigation models as part of the Joint National Action Plan and the roll-out of Operation Soteria as part of the End-to-End Rape Review.

94   Home Office data, 2020.

least a one- or two-year wait between someone being charged with rape and the case going to trial. Trial dates are often changed or delayed at the last minute, with no real thought about the impact on the victim. Another year without a chance to see your attacker in court is another year in stasis for most.

But it's not just the wait times and being treated like a suspect that causes victims to drop out, although these are probably the two most important factors. They are simply worn down by every interaction with the criminal justice system. From the woman behind the counter at the Haven in London where I went for my forensic medical exam, popping bubbles with her gum, gossiping and giggling behind the reception desk, to police officers not returning phone calls or emails with requests for updates, to being told your case just isn't a priority, to the CPS sending letters to rape victims that are so abysmal and inhumane that they've been subject to two Inspectorate reviews that found them woefully inadequate, but still the desire can't be found to change them.

Victims are treated as though they are bothersome utility customers. If you want water in your home, you have to let the water company treat you however they want. It's often not great, but you have no choice (and it's usually significantly better than going to court). Imagine every neutral-to-negative customer service interaction you've ever had, and understand it's far better than the way rape victims are treated, by everyone from the Sexual Assault Referral Centre (where your forensic medical exam happens) to the police, to the CPS; where it's not even considered a priority to provide victims with support in court, or even to provide a waiting room that's separate and secure from their attackers; where Witness Services treat everyone waiting the same way, whether they're a witness or a victim. Throughout every stage of the entire system, most victims are treated as though they don't matter, as though their experience doesn't matter, as though they're not worth the effort or empathy that's required to deal with them.

There is, of course, a question of money. Budgets are, as always, finite, but I tend to think it's also a failure of empathy, a complete inability to understand what it is to be a victim of a crime, let alone a victim of rape. We're humans, we've had this horrible thing happen to us, and while going to court or being in a police station might just be any day at the office for you, the professional, rape was likely the worst day or days of our lives. And if you treat us worse than a customer with a question about a water bill, perhaps you need to take a long hard look in the mirror.

That said, more money would help to fund training for police on trauma responses in victims and investigation techniques for rape that have worked in other countries or in pilot areas here in the UK. Training would also be helpful for the CPS in countering rape myths and dealing empathetically with victims. Professional victim support services should be provided: we shouldn't need to rely on volunteers and well-meaning amateurs, but on mental health professionals trained in PTSD and trauma stress responses; courthouses and services should recognise that for every serious crime, there is a victim.

Meanwhile in the Witness Waiting Room, we continued to listen to the CPS prosecutor speaking to the other victim. Eventually, I snapped. I borrowed a pen and a piece of lined notebook paper from

Gavin, wrote down my lawyer's details, and stood up and walked across the room to give it to the victim, to let her know that she might be able to get some help, particularly if she wanted to know what her options were; at the very least, that having her own lawyer might help her in dealing with the CPS.

It probably wasn't my finest moment, but in full stress mode with PTSD flaring at the edges, my irrational response was a need to help: to make the prosecutor stop treating her in such a horrible manner; to help her get the justice she deserved; to not see her case being flushed away by an uncaring prosecutor who would not or could not understand her or her situation.

Not long after that, the obviously irritated prosecutor showed her into a consultation room to continue their conversation in private, and that was the last I saw of them. Moments later a Witness Room Attendant came in to let me know it was time.

We stood and wove our way through the labyrinthine hallways and staircases from the Witness Waiting Room to the courtroom.

I entered and was directed to the witness box. True enough, there was a little stand-up book with the oath printed on it. I was asked to stand to read it out. The courtroom was brightly lit, and unlike the dark-panelled court for the criminal appeal case, eight and a half months earlier, the judge's bench and my witness box were made of what looked almost like Ikea furniture: totally functional, a light-coloured wood that may or may not have been particle board. I was seated behind a screen, one of the options available to vulnerable and intimidated witnesses. I could also have pre-recorded my statement or had someone else read it out in court, but, even given my wobble in the early hours of the morning, I felt like my story was most powerful coming from my mouth, in person. I needed to feel that I'd made my case, and also, after the previous five years, I honestly didn't trust the CPS to make my case for me.

I wanted to feel safe. I wanted to do all I could do to make sure that John was on the sex offenders register and that he'd never be able to contact me again. It was my hope that with all these elements in place, I could start to feel some sense of safety again. I wanted to feel like I could exert some element of control over proceedings, even if that just meant turning up.

From behind the barrier I could only see the judge and John's solicitor. I couldn't see the CPS prosecutor on my case, Varinder Hayre, nor anyone in the gallery. Most importantly, I couldn't see John. I didn't know that there were a number of members of the press in the gallery again, and that this time, John had brought his mother to court. I can only imagine this was because he was now facing the possibility of jail time, or that he wanted her to give evidence of what she thought was his good character. Perhaps she just felt he was a good boy who took care of her: his solicitor had told the court he was her carer. Like the families and friends of many people accused of sexual assault, perhaps she took John at his word and thought it had just been a misunderstanding.

I began to read out my Victim Personal Statement, trying not to let my voice catch as I skipped over the redacted sections. My knees shook as I tried not to cry. A few more sections had been marked with a pen; John's solicitor had objected to the part saying he'd masturbated *over* me. It was changed to "next to", but he seemed to accept that the masturbation had actually taken place, and therefore that he'd probably broken the law.

Chapter Seven

After the large blacked-out section, I continued to read it aloud and onto the record. "What happened that evening five years ago changed my life almost completely," I said. "After leaving that hotel room back in May of 2015, my world fell apart. That evening I had a hyperventilating panic attack for the first time in my life. That was just the start: in the end I had a total breakdown and was diagnosed with post-traumatic stress disorder as a result of the incident. PTSD is not some faddy, subjective state of mind, it is a serious condition that can even be seen in an MRI. All I know, is it nearly killed me. On March 1, 2016, I went back to the same hotel where Mr Doe filmed me naked and attempted suicide. I am lucky to be here today." I paused.

Collecting myself, I continued: "After my suicide attempt, I sought intensive treatment, and was in regular therapy working through my trauma and stress responses. A couple of months later, although I was not remotely close to being cured, I was on track for recovery. That recovery was completely derailed on May 25, 2016, when the police sat me down to finally tell me about the video. I had no idea the video existed until then. It was a physical blow. I had to leave the room and I thought I was going to be sick. The panic attacks came back and I suffered a relapse in my PTSD symptoms. I was rehospitalised that July and at the end of the year, I was made redundant from my job. I never have been able to secure a full-time role since. That is why, to me, this offence is not trivial," I said. Another blacked-out section.

"To find out that this man had taken a video of me naked and that I was unaware of this for more than a year made me even more anxious and very mistrustful of people around me. Not knowing why he did it and what he has done with my image, including potentially sharing it privately or publicly, made me feel like my privacy and personal space had been violently invaded. Even now I do not know for certain where my body had been seen and by whom and, realising that he and maybe others could have repeatedly looked at me in my most vulnerable state – naked and asleep – has made me feel violated over and over again.

"I cannot overstate what the voyeurism offence specifically has done to me in terms of my physical and mental health. Feelings of anxiety and mistrustfulness have had a dramatic and highly negative effect on my ability to continue with my professional and personal life. My career is only now beginning to get back on track, and as a result I have missed out on tens of thousands of pounds of income which could have led to an easier and better life for my daughter. And for a very long time, for years, I found it almost impossible to form and maintain friendships and deeper relationships, adding to my sense of loneliness and anxiety. Taking the video of me may, at first glance, seem to be trivial and easily dismissed, a 62-second aberration. But it is in reality profoundly disturbing, debilitating and ultimately devastating. The fact that he did it within the context of his actions that night makes it all the more painful."

I paused. There were seven more blacked-out lines.

"What he has done," I concluded, "his voyeurism, has ruined my life."

I sat at the end of my statement, folding the sheets together again. The court went on to discuss other matters. Most of that didn't register and my memory is largely a blur. I heard some small particulars of my attacker's life, like that he was currently unemployed and staying with his mother while living off his savings. Mention of medical things. The irregular and unexpected costs of maintaining an elderly pet. I sat, alone and withdrawn, behind the screen, folding in on myself.

The judge then asked for John's finance form and the court ground to a halt when it turned out that it hadn't been filled in yet. I sat behind the screen for what felt like an hour before being led through the courthouse's hallways and staircases, back to the Witness Waiting Room.

It was a nerve-wrecking pause. Everything sat in the judge's hands.

Chapter Eight

People have a hard time believing that rape happens as often as it does, or in the ways that it does. As discussed earlier, the very human desire to prefer to believe that women lie about rape rather than men actually commit it is exactly that: very human. And of course, the police who investigate rape and the prosecutors who decide whether to charge or not are human.

Humans are fallible. Police officers are no different.[95]

As we waited for the judge to come back, I couldn't help but think about the morning after

---

[95] https://kb.osu.edu/bitstream/handle/1811/73188/OSJCL_V8N1_007.pdf?sequence=1

I was raped, when two female police officers sat side by side in straight-backed chairs, notebooks in hand, the pale sunshine just filtering into my living room through the window behind them. Nicola and Caroline[96] began to ask questions. I hadn't really been able to understand Nicola when she'd phoned me that morning. I wasn't hungover, but I still wasn't feeling exactly right either. The world had a fuzziness to it, so when she suggested coming by later in the day, it felt like the right move. She'd seemed abrupt, abrasive even, but I'd chalked it up to a bad connection and my state of mind.

I sat curled in the corner of my couch with my feet pulled under me, leaning against the arm for support. I was alone, utterly alone, and they started firing away, prompting and nudging me to uncover the story of what happened the day before.

As I went through the parts I could remember, I explained that I was sure I was drugged, not least because if I'd drunk enough alcohol to have a five-hour blackout, I would have been violently ill. I explained that something had been very wrong, that I was very upset, that I was very scared.

---

96   Names have been changed.

Chapter Eight

They asked a few questions as I told my story and Caroline scribbled away in her notebook. When I was done, Nicola spoke to me.

"You know, we don't actually have to do the report. We know how it is."

She lowered her voice in that slightly conspiratorial way that people you don't know use to help you understand that they get you, that they are on your side.

"Know how it is?" I asked, confused.

"You have a bit too much to drink," Nicola started, "and then one thing leads to another and you hook up with someone. Your boyfriend got upset, so…"

I started to shake. I expect that the blood drained from my face. Something was very wrong. This police officer, to whom I'd just told my whole story, thought I was making it up.

"I…" I paused. "I don't have a boyfriend," I said, trying to make her understand. Admittedly, it probably wasn't the strongest counter-argument. But I was at a total loss. I was stunned.

"No one will know that you decided not to file the report," she continued. "You wouldn't get into trouble."

"I want to file the report," I said plainly. "But I don't know what happened. I don't even know if we had sex. He said we didn't and I don't know. I was drugged and woke up naked in a hotel room."

Then it was Caroline's turn. "Right, well, we're going to need to take your phone with us."

"Excuse me?"

"We need to have the tech guys go through it," she said.

"I can't be without my phone right now, I need to be able to reach people."

"Right, well give it here and I can take some notes."

I handed Caroline my phone, and she started to go through my texts. Then she started to write down the phone number of the lawyer I was supposed to have met for dinner for a first date the night before.

"Wait, what are you doing?" I asked.

"Writing down this guy's number."

"No! You can't just contact people I know. I haven't told a lot of people what happened. I don't want people to know."

"Well, if you want to file this report, then we're going to have to talk to this person. And your dad. And anyone else you contacted last night."

Chapter Eight

"But I don't want people to know that I was raped."

"It's up to you. You don't have to file the report after all," she said, to my silence. My breath became ragged again as tears began to stream down my face.

At that moment the doorbell rang and my friend Kitty arrived, just in time to intervene. She asked Caroline and Nicola to wait outside while she calmed me down. She gave me a huge hug, sat me down in the kitchen and started making tea.

She went back out to the police while I drank the tea and asked them to wait another 20 minutes for me to catch my breath and get my bearings. They opted to leave instead, said they'd be in touch and that I should let them know if I wanted to file the report and then be seen by the Haven.

Kitty hung my hammock in the back garden and settled me down with a blanket and the tea. I watched the clouds and tried not to think, swaying lightly in the breeze. Kitty sat nearby, working away on her laptop, checking on me every so often.

I had a huge decision to make. The police quite clearly weren't with me; they didn't believe me, or something else was wrong. I felt unsupported, disbelieved. I also felt repeatedly violated. I had no idea what had happened to me, but the police were the ones making me feel even more unsettled. Nicola's tone on the phone that morning came back to me, as did the way she and Caroline looked at me – unfeeling, unsympathetic, disbelieving. Could I really go through with filing the report and submitting to a forensic medical examination? Having the most intimate parts of my body examined by a stranger while all the intimate parts of my life would be examined by the police?

Kitty brought out another in what had become an endless supply of mugs of tea, and then hopped into the hammock with me. We swung for the split second that the hammock stayed in the air – until the garden fence toppled inward and we landed with two thuds on the ground, covered in tea and laughing.

As the laughter subsided, Kitty asked what I was going to do. And I had decided. I decided to believe the stranger in the hotel room. I decided to believe that maybe nothing had happened. He'd had all of his clothes on after all. And he'd said that nothing happened. The police told me that when he was arrested, he'd said that nothing had happened. And I didn't want to deal with the police anymore.

At 5:00pm, just over 24 hours after my last memory before I woke up naked next to a stranger, I headed upstairs, stripped off my clothes and turned on my shower as hot as I could stand. Slowly, methodically, I washed away all the evidence of the night before, all of the fear, all of the panic, all of the worry, all of the decision-making. I washed it all away. And said goodbye to it. Because I hoped that it was over, that nothing had happened, that there was nothing left to do. And with the police acting the way they were, on balance, I chose to believe that nothing had happened.

In that moment, I briefly became a statistic, one of the 58% of victims in a reported rape who stop participating in their case.[97] I gave up. And it was as a direct result of the way I'd been treated: disbelieved and discouraged.

In a study of detectives and specialist sexual offence liaison officers in an unnamed police force in England, researchers found there was a huge variance across officers over how often they believed

97   Home Office data, 2020. Up from 42% five years earlier.

women lied about rape, from an officer believing that women lie about rape 5% of the time to another believing it was 90% of the time.[98] The average across the force was 53%. By contrast, an independent analysis of their files found that around 3.4% of cases reported to them might have been false: much higher than what other studies had found, but still much less than even the lowest estimate by police officers (5%) of how often women lie about rape.

Many of the police officers in this study told the researchers how they just know if someone is telling the truth, that it's their gut or their "copper's nose".[99] They claimed that inconsistency in a victim's story[100] was the main clue to an allegation being false.

---

98 McMillan, L. (2018) "Police officers' perceptions of false allegations of rape", *Journal of Gender Studies*, vol. 27, no. 1, pp. 9–21. https://doi.org/10.1080/09589236.2016.1194260

99 *ibid.*

100 In re-reading the statement that I gave to the police in May 2015, it doesn't sound like me: the order of events isn't as I remember it and it doesn't reflect a lot of what I now know. This is partly because of the impact of trauma on memory, partly that I've spent years trying to work through what happened to me, and, unfortunately, partly because the police officers had no compassion for me and didn't understand my trauma responses in the days following the assault.

Chapter Eight

Every police officer is likely aware that eye-witness accounts are notoriously unreliable. Since criminologist Franz von Liszt's 1902 experiment, when he staged a classroom fight and shooting to discover that his students' written accounts of the event were widely inaccurate,[101] study after study has shown that people get the details of crimes wrong.[102] That is, they get the details of crimes they see happening wrong – and that's when they aren't even the victim and haven't just endured a horrifying or traumatic experience. Not knowing the exact order of events, or the precise time some happened, or getting confused, or, as in my case, having a panic attack or disassociating, are all widely recognised patterns of behaviour after a traumatic event. I wonder, if there were enough false allegation cases to study – and there probably aren't – whether they could be picked apart to determine if there is a slightly higher correlation between a consistent story and it being false.

---

101 Münsterberg, Hugo (1908). *On the Witness Stand*. (The McClure Company).
102 http://www.desksgt.com/Classes/Reading/uncorrobo-rated_eyewitness_id.pdf

Which is not to say that a consistent story makes a rape allegation false, just that if someone were going to make it up, surely they'd be more likely to get their false facts and details straight before reporting it.

Somehow, police officers are relying on their "copper's nose" to determine if rape victims are lying, and justifying their gut feeling by demanding a higher level of consistency and accuracy from a victim's statement than from a mere witness.

Why does this happen? I suspect it partly becomes apparent when we look at what happens in general when people overestimate their own abilities. In 1999, Professors David Dunning and Justin Kruger published a stunning finding: people in the bottom quartile of a variety of assessments massively overestimated their abilities.[103] Dunning and Kruger reported that the participants made poor choices and drew the wrong conclusions and that, even worse, their "incompetence robs them of the metacognitive ability to realize it."[104] Essentially, the less people

---

103   https://www.avaresearch.com/files/UnskilledAnd-UnawareOfIt.pdf
104   *ibid.*

know, the more they think they know. This became known as the Dunning–Kruger Effect.

When we apply the Dunning–Kruger Effect to the way police often investigate rape, we can immediately see there's a problem.

In the L. Macmillan study quoted above, investigating police officers overall believed that women lied about rape 53% of the time: a huge contrast to the estimate that up to 2–3% of rape allegations in this country are false. As a result, we can quite firmly conclude that these police officers knew much less about rape and rape victims than they thought they did. Because of this lack of knowledge, they are likely to be making poor choices and drawing erroneous conclusions in their investigations.

If police officers believe that they have a preternatural "lie detector" ability, but also believe that women lie about rape by default, they are likely to make objectively wrong and essentially incompetent decisions while investigating rape. And this lack of real knowledge and expertise will simply be reinforced over the years by this false belief in their own ability or their "copper's nose" to simply just know the truth. It becomes self-reinforcing. The

Dunning–Kruger research showed that those with greater abilities are more likely to doubt them. Indeed, any police officer who believes in their ability to simply know the truth, above and beyond the evidence, is almost certainly suffering from the Dunning–Kruger Effect.

Officers in the L. Macmillan study were also making judgements on the truthfulness of a rape victim based on what they saw as her motivation for making the complaint: trying to get back at someone, or regretting an encounter for example.[105] Those officers who believed that victims lie about rape regularly said that women were maliciously making false accusations. Indeed, if there was a conflict between ex-partners – over custody or finances, for example – it could be a police officer's first leap: there's a motivation to lie, so she must be lying. One female detective said to the researchers, "I think she was being vindictive and trying to get him back, because he said he was taking her to court

---

105   McMillan, L. (2018) "Police officers' perceptions of false allegations of rape", *Journal of Gender Studies*, vol. 27, no. 1, pp. 9–21. https://doi.org/10.1080/09589236.2016.1194260

for a share of the house."[106] In reality, this is most likely to be the wrong way of looking at it. Instead, it's much more likely that the man in question did indeed rape his ex-partner. But that's not how the case was viewed.

Research has borne out that false rape allegations, which do exist but are incredibly rare, don't look like the sorts of cases that the police officers in the study thought were false. For example, when a journalist reviewed a number of studies on rape allegations, he discovered that one of the most common situations was when a "teenage girl tells her parents she was raped to avoid getting in trouble".[107] It is then not surprising that two different studies found that nearly 50% of false rape allegations are rapes reported by someone other than the alleged victim, often the parent of a teenage girl.

In other genuine cases of fabricated rape allegations, there is usually a pattern of "bizarre fabrications or criminal fraud".[108] Before someone

---

106 *ibid.*
107 https://qz.com/980766/the-truth-about-false-rape-accusations/
108 *ibid.*

makes up an allegation of rape, they've made up many other things, which they've also brought to the police. However, the police officers in the L. Macmillan study seemed unaware of this, choosing instead to believe that the majority of female rape victims are making up their story.

As infrequent as false rape allegations are, it is also important to note that they almost never result in prison time for the falsely accused. While there is no relevant dataset for this in the UK, in the first 30 years since records on criminal exonerations began in the USA (1989), only 52 men were jailed for sexual assaults they were subsequently found to be innocent of. To provide some context, over that same period, 790 people were found not to have committed the murder they were convicted of.

And yet, the police are all too ready to treat rape victims as if they're the ones who've committed a crime. Far too many rape victims end up being the suspect in the eyes of officers. And, as mentioned earlier, the rape victims have historically been investigated first, before the police examine the crime or the suspect.

There is hope, however; the Dunning–Kruger research discovered that when confronted with new and genuine knowledge, these participants began to see their limitations.[109] The greatest proof that they had learned something? Admitting that they didn't know everything.

The police rang me again two days after I was raped.

"He has admitted to the sex, but says it was consensual," Nicola said. I felt the warm phone pressed against my cheek starting to slip as my jaw dropped and my fingers loosened. "We interviewed him yesterday," she continued, as I tried to re-orientate myself.

"There was sex?" I asked, stunned and not taking anything in.

"Yes, but he says it was consensual."

"How can it have been consensual if I can't remember it?"

Nicola continued to speak, but I couldn't really hear any of it. I was standing in the American Embassy, renewing my daughter's passport and trying to hide in a corner while having what was

109 https://www.avaresearch.com/files/UnskilledAnd-UnawareOfIt.pdf

turning out to be a deeply personal phone conversation. The police were just telling me, in a rather matter-of-fact manner, that I had indeed been raped and that the stranger in the hotel room had lied to me two days earlier when he'd said nothing had happened. John was officially my rapist. What little hope I'd had, whatever story I'd told myself about the basic decency of people, whatever I'd wanted to believe, was gone.

Also, the police had known since the night before but had decided not to tell me until then. It suddenly occurred to me that none of the things that should have happened immediately – a forensic examination, the morning-after pill, HIV prophylaxis – had happened. And there was a ticking clock on all of them. Worse, I had let the police bully me into not filing a report. I had showered. My mind whirled with panic.

"I need to be seen by the Haven, today," I said, probably at a random point in the conversation. I literally couldn't process what Nicola was saying.

"I can call them, but they might not have an appointment for you today."

"I need to be seen by the Haven, today," I

repeated. "I have childcare and support this afternoon at 2:00pm, that's when I can go."

"That's not how it works, Emily," Nicola said, the nasty tone returning to her voice. Every time she said my name it sounded like nails on a chalkboard. She called me by name whenever she was trying to make a point I didn't want to hear, either a verbal tic or the result of some really poorly received victim-support training. It didn't make me feel listened to; it made me feel that after the worst thing that had ever happened to me, this person, who was supposed to be providing support, really didn't care that I existed or had any needs or concerns that deserved her attention.

"Look," I said, starting to lose my patience. "You've just told me that I was raped. It's two days later. I need to see the Haven and I need to see them today. I need to be checked out, I need to get the morning-after pill, I need…" I was aware that my voice was rising and that people were starting to stare.

"There were used condoms in the hotel room, so you're probably fine. It's up to the Haven if they see you…"

I cut in. "Wait, what?! There were used condoms in the hotel room and no one thought to tell me until right now that I'd actually been raped? Did he say that he used one the whole time? Does he have any STDs? How do I know…"

"Well, Emily, we don't have to tell you anything about what we've found at the scene, this call is a courtesy call…" Nicola interrupted. Her voice was rising, her tone getting nastier. And then she started yelling at me.

I didn't need to be informed that I'd been raped. It wasn't the police's job to inform me. And I should settle down because they weren't going to tell me anything else.

I again insisted that I be connected with the Haven; Nicola said she'd call them and would let me know if they wanted to see me. If.

I went through the bureaucratic motions of renewing the passport. Went to first one window, then another. My reflection was pale and drawn. I looked tired. The defeat was showing clearly. It used to be that you couldn't bring mobile phones into the American Embassy, and in between each window and each form, I sat in hard plastic chairs thinking about what it would be like to not know, to believe for just a little bit longer that perhaps I hadn't been raped. That perhaps the police's mistreatment of me and the hospital's lack of treatment wouldn't matter because it had all been some misunderstanding.

There's a chasm between what I thought the police's role should have been when they turned up at the hotel that night and what they believed it to be. As mentioned earlier, rape seems to be treated differently than any other crime, in that the investigation is usually "victim-centric". That doesn't mean what I naively thought it should mean: that the victim and their needs are put at the centre of the investigation. What it means in practice is that the investigation begins with the victim: with their story and their credibility being pulled apart. There's no initial examination of the suspect; in fact, to this day, I'm not aware that the police have conducted any sort of investigation into John. They didn't look at his digital footprint beyond the video he took of me on his phone and didn't use technological experts to ascertain whether or not he'd shared or uploaded the video until I asked them to, over a year later. They didn't look into the fact he was found with illegal drugs, or whether he could have had access to a date-rape drug like GHB by virtue of having access to other illicit substances. I'm fairly certain they didn't look into his background or try to determine whether he had a history of taking advantage of women who he thought might be on drugs or mentally ill.[110]

Instead, they looked at me. And I was a mess. I was deeply traumatised and, apparently, to them, doing all the wrong things. My timeline was likely confused as I was missing a five-hour chunk of time. I didn't want to tell people I knew that I'd been raped. Instead of trying to get Nicola and Caroline to like me, I made demands – like wanting medical attention and to know what was happening with my case – that felt very obvious to me, but made them think I was making it all up. Fundamentally, I was displaying the text-book behaviour of someone having a traumatic stress response. They were acting like it was any day at the office and I was a pain they were stuck dealing with who was getting in the way

---

110   An outcome of Project Bluestone in Avon & Somerset (2021) was that police forces around the country were advised to consider beginning a rape investigation by running background checks on named rape suspects. Previously, the suspect's name wasn't run through a database until the end of the investigation, if it even got that far.

of their routine.[111] I was doing the wrong things and, quickly, wasn't credible and thus wasn't worthy.

By overestimating their "copper's nose" ability to know which women are lying about rape, police officers fall into the same rape-myth trap and obsession with false rape allegations as other people.

Except they are the gatekeepers of the criminal justice system.

There have been countless attempts to reform the way the police deal with rape victims. In fact, when my rape was reported to the Metropolitan Police in London, formal guidelines existed instructing police officers to start from a position of believing rape victims (unbelievably, this policy was scrapped in April 2018).

Regardless, it often seems to come down to whether a victim is likeable or not, whether their rape story is "believable" and whether the police

---

111   As mentioned in Chapter One, I made a complaint to the IOPC about the way the police treated me in the first week after John was reported for suspicion of rape. The IOPC found that the police acted entirely appropriately. The report that they sent following an investigation that took more than a year misspelled my surname and had other details wrong. There was no way to appeal, other than to bring a judicial review. It didn't seem worth the fight.

consider it a priority or not. What it doesn't come down to is the humanity of the rape victim, the provable fact that the police are wrong about how often women lie about rape, that false rape allegations are rare and that most rapes happen between people who know each other.

Police are people too, but until we recognise that any police officer who believes that women lie about rape[112] is likely to make incompetent decisions, rape victims will be let down at the first hurdle. The Dunning–Kruger Effect provides the hint: if, through training, the police don't realise they still have a lot to learn about the realities of rape, rape victims, trauma responses and how rape myths colour their world view, then they're not ready to be involved in rape investigations.

Having eventually been through a forensic medical examination the week after I was raped, I sometimes think that those who rail about false rape allegations – from the police to the Twittersphere – should have an examination themselves, to better understand that just about no one would go through that experience by choice. If the police had chosen

---

112   There are a variety of objective measurement criteria for this.

to believe me at the outset, gathered the evidence and considered John's damning police statement from a suspect-focused point of view, I could have been waiting for sentencing for an altogether different charge.

Chapter Nine

"The facts of this case are shocking," said District Judge Ciecióra to the hushed courtroom. Afraid to look up, I watched my fingers run over the top of the small desk inside the witness box as though they were someone else's. This was the moment I'd fought five long years for, the moment when John would face at least some consequences for his actions that night. Though I couldn't see him through the screen enclosing me and protecting me from the gaze of the rest of the courtroom, I knew that John was standing just a few feet away, awaiting his fate.

"You knew it was morally wrong and deceitful to record an intimate video," the judge continued.

"You prioritised your own desires without any real thought of how it would affect the victim."[113]

Scenes from the previous five years danced through my memory. From waking up terrified next to John, to finding out about the video, to the CPS insisting that John hadn't committed any crime, to meeting Kate, to changing the law on voyeurism, to all of the heartache and heartbreak along the way, to the reality of making it as far as sitting in that box, trying to stay grounded in the moment by feeling the texture of the desk under my fingertips. I fought to not disappear into the whirl of memories and images. I looked up at the judge.

"While the merits of this case meet the custodial threshold, you were awarded a discount on your sentence for pleading guilty at the first possible opportunity."

And then, just like that, it was over. No jail time.

I guess I'd always sort of thought that would happen. Regardless, I felt tears well up in my eyes as I told myself that the fear of jail had probably been

---

113   https://www.standard.co.uk/news/crime/hotel-stranger-emily-hunt-naked-prosecution-justice-east-london-a4540531.html

punishment enough. I had what I most wanted: some recognition of the fact that what John did was wrong. And as the judge continued to deliver her judgement, it became clear that she did absolutely recognise that.

He was sentenced to what the judge described as a substantial community order, meaning he'd have a probation officer for as long as the order was in place and would need to follow all the rules that the judge or the probation service imposed on him. She gave him a 30-month-long community order and ordered him to attend a sex offenders' rehabilitation programme.

"Would he prefer a fine or a curfew?" the judge asked John's solicitor.

"A fine," she replied, without missing a beat.

The blood rushed to my face. I wanted to scream, I wanted to jump out of my seat in the witness box, I wanted someone to listen to me. Deep down, irrationally or not, I desperately wanted John's liberty curtailed. I wanted there to be an impact on his life. I wanted him to at least be unable to leave his house when he wanted, just as I'd been unable to leave my house when he caused a flare-up of my

PTSD symptoms in July. But what I wanted wasn't ever going to matter: no one was listening. I was alone in the box, shaking. Isolated from Kate and Gavin, not even able to see the CPS prosecutor.

The rules of giving a Victim Personal Statement prevent the victim from being allowed to say what sort of punishment they want: that's for the objective court to decide. But what I knew rationally didn't change how my body felt, as my mind spun and those small pieces of victory and control seemed to fall between my fingers into some far-off depth.

I fought for the surface while the judge and John's solicitor talked back and forth about the sentence, and the solicitor pushed for the length of the community order to be reduced.

"But the original probation service report recommended 18 months," said the solicitor.

My whirling thoughts began to slow. I wiped a tear from the corner of my eye and started to focus in on the conversation.

"Both the probation service and I agree that he is at high likelihood of reoffending," said the judge. "While he has expressed regret for his actions, Mr Doe has not shown remorse for them."

My jaw dropped. High likelihood of reoffending.

In addition to the community order, John was given a fine, ordered to pay me £5,000 in compensation and to pay the court costs. He was placed on the sex offenders register for five years and I was given an indefinite restraining order against him.

I fought for five years to have John see the inside of a courtroom. In that time, I'd sacrificed my career, relationships with friends and family who didn't understand, my time and, at various points, my mental wellbeing, to be sitting in that courtroom. I'd fought against police officers who told me that sometimes these things just happen, and I'd been forced to stand up to prosecutors who lied to me and who told me over and over that John had done nothing wrong. I had to raise money to bring a case against the CPS in court to force a change in the law.

I had to do all of it.

And I nearly stopped so many times because I was broken by it all. But I'd finally done it: he'd finally been convicted of a sex offence, all because I'd fought for it.

Without my efforts, though, John would not have a criminal record. The next person he would have done this to would either have had to take on this fight themselves or just give up. As the judge said, John prioritised his own desires without any consideration of what the victim wanted. This is, as discussed in Chapter Six, exactly what researchers have shown makes a rapist a rapist: wanting to have sex with someone who either hasn't given consent or is incapable of giving consent, and then having sex with them anyway.

Whatever John thought about our encounter that night in May 2015, regardless of what was said between us when we met, John had thought that I was either mentally ill or on drugs, and, at the very least, knew I was so intoxicated that I was unable to stand up on my own as we entered the hotel room. He was sober. Any reasonable, sober person should have known that I couldn't have consented to anything in that state.[114]

He had sex with me regardless. He masturbated onto me while I was unconscious because he wanted

---

114 In a review of my case in response to a complaint that I brought against the CPS in spring 2021, they reiterated that they did not believe there was sufficient evidence to charge John with rape. Furthermore, they told my lawyers that CCTV evidence of me kissing John in the street on the way to the hotel would, essentially, amount to consent for sex in the eyes of a jury.

to. He took a video of my naked body, knowing full well it was wrong, because he felt entitled to ignore my lack of consent or my inability to give consent. He had no remorse for any of it. He regretted that I fought for justice; he regretted being in the courtroom; he regretted the consequences, even if they were, in the grand scheme of things, small consequences.

I was shown out of the courtroom and escorted back to the Witness Waiting Room by Paul and one of the attendants. The hallways were a blur. Actually, everything was a blur. I couldn't focus or even really figure out how I felt. It was over. John wasn't going to jail. His liberty hadn't really been affected at all. But he was on the sex offenders register and could never contact me again. It felt incomplete.

Back in the sun-filled room, I decided I couldn't do any press interviews. How could I tell people how I felt when I didn't know? Gavin wrote out a draft of a statement for me, and Kate went to read it out to the press who were waiting outside. They bustled about and I sat, full of stillness. Empty.

Dressed in her dark and conservative court-room outfit, Varinder, the prosecutor, came into the waiting room to go over everything. She explained that the long community order would mean that John would actually have substantially more oversight than if he'd received a jail sentence, whether actually served in jail or suspended. The maximum jail sentence would have possibly only been a couple of months, followed by a less intrusive probation. Thirty months of a community order would mean that John would be restricted by strident rules for a long enough time to hopefully make a difference. I smiled, trying to engage. I thanked her.

"I'm just so sorry that this happened to you, Emily," Varinder said, her voice starting to crack. Her eyes began to glisten. "I was supposed to be on holiday this week," she continued. "But I wanted to be here to get something for you." A tear slid down her cheek.

I leapt up from the couch and, after speeding across the room, hugged her. Somehow, the crying prosecutor, the first person I'd encountered in the CPS or police who seemed to care about not just my case but getting justice for victims, made the victory feel a bit less hollow.

That afternoon I was half asleep in the passenger seat of the car as Gavin steered through the edges of London. I was escaping the city for a night, just to be in a different place and put some physical space between the last five years and me. Hanging out with my friend at his cottage in the countryside seemed like exactly the right sort of medicine for the moment. A pub-garden supper and champagne awaited us on the other side of the traffic. At the top of the hour, the BBC news bulletin started. I was the first story. It was from the interview I'd filmed the day before, but it felt like a year before. It felt like listening to a different person, from a different time.

"You do know you've really changed things, right?" Gavin asked.

When I first started doing press interviews in October 2017, my motivation was purely mercenary. I wanted two things: to raise money to see John prosecuted and to change the conversation around sexual violence. Over time, the second purpose became the most important to me.

It came down to the simple fact that in so many interactions, whether with people in my life or even my run-ins with the criminal justice system, the same misconceptions seemed to pop up over and over again. The same rape myths, the same ideas that rape is rare, that women lie about it, that drinking or wearing a short skirt or flirting or any number of other things make a victim culpable in their own rape. When the CPS says that they don't think there's a realistic prospect of conviction and drop a rape case, more often than not it's because they think people cannot move beyond these same old hackneyed victim blaming ideas. The only solution is to change the way we talk about it.

But fundamentally, it's hugely difficult to have conversations about sexual violence because it's a fraught and complicated subject, loaded with issues around sex and sexuality, people's roles and expectations in society and maybe even a bit of guilt. It's even more difficult because we're hardwired to not want to believe that rape happens, let alone as often as it does – and everyone responds to trauma differently.

In the year before I went public with my rape, Claire,[115] a family friend visiting from out of town,

---

115   Some details have been changed to protect identities. As with the earlier story about "Luke", this isn't about the individual or the actions described here – it's about this being really normal behaviour which victims sometimes face from their family and friends. This isn't a person to be identified, or named and shamed. It's a story aimed at recognising and confronting this very human behaviour in ourselves and the people around us.

stayed on my couch from time to time while applying for jobs in London after university. It was nice
to have the company and my daughter loved having
her around. We cheered each other up when the
other was down, I donated most of a work wardrobe
to her out of hand-me-downs from the back of my
closet, and sometimes she'd turn off my bedroom
light if I fell asleep reading.

She moved into her own flat near mine not long
before I started speaking in public about what had
happened to me, and things got so intense for me
at that time that it took me a while to notice that
she'd sort of disappeared from my life. She'd pop up
every once in a while to ask to pick up my daughter
from school and have her over for supper, but we
never hung out. I just assumed we were both busy.

But actually she disappeared the very moment
I started talking out loud about my experience.
Perhaps I was making too much of it; perhaps she
felt I should move on or that I wasn't worth her time.
When it turned out she was telling anyone we knew
in common how horrible I was or how toxic I was
or how everyone should cut me out of their lives, I
was devastated. I hadn't expected to be let down in

that way and definitely hadn't expected that sort of vitriol to be directed at me. I was just trying to get through life day by day.

When I look back on the situation, of course, I fully recognise that, in the throes of PTSD, I was complicated and broken and probably seemed pretty toxic much of the time. The year before I started speaking publicly about rape, I spent a lot of time working on my stress responses, trying to manage them and prevent being held hostage by my symptoms. But it was imperfect. I was deeply imperfect. And any interaction with the criminal justice system or my attacker made my symptoms worse.

The reality is that people I knew responded to my talking about rape with their own internal judgement, values and baggage. For all I know, Claire needed to feel that my rape was my fault, because otherwise something like this could happen to her or someone she cared about. Maybe something like this had already happened to her and she'd told herself the story that it was her fault, and my making a big deal about what had happened to me and demanding justice rattled her own narrative. Maybe it was just my fault for trusting the wrong person.

But the reasons don't really matter: a similar thing happened to me with a few other people, and I've since heard similar stories from other rape victims.

The situation with Claire, in much the same way as when my friendship with my Pilates teacher Luke fell apart,[116] did make it much clearer for me that when having conversations with the people around us about sexual violence, the layers of personal experiences and world views can become either a bridge, or a wall.

I recently asked a few friends about what my speaking out had done for them, or if I'd had any impact. I wanted to know if there'd been a positive aspect for those who stuck by me by being part of my story and my support circle – even the wide and impersonal support of friends online. A number of replies said that I didn't really change much for them: they already knew that rape was an unrecognised issue; others said they'd never really understood the landscape until they came into contact with me; many were somewhere in between.[117]

---

116 See Chapter Four.

117 It isn't lost on me that two out of the three examples I share below are people I met after May 2015, while the third is

Kat wrote that she'd first seen me on TV talking about my case and trying to obtain justice. When I asked her about it, she said, "I remember feeling like I had an ally, someone who understood what I was going through. I felt terribly sad that you'd not had justice, while I was feeling positive about getting my rapist convicted. When they dropped my case, I realised I was now a member of the failed justice club and my heart broke knowing this was how you'd felt too."

For Kat I was a fellow traveller, someone with lived experience of being raped and being let down by the system. I'd thought that beyond sharing my story, there was nothing else I could give her, but then she told me: "I didn't realise the staggering numbers affected by the lack of charging and conviction. Your stats and storytelling have often given me the platform to start these conversations... It's got those outside of our circle talking."

My favourite teacher from secondary school, Linda, told me: "Watching your efforts over the

---

someone I hadn't really reconnected with until after the assault. Going through rape is hard, and it's also really hard to be part of the support network for someone who's been raped.

past few years, I realised that perseverance and justice go hand in hand! You were harmed in horrible ways and the justice system did not want to recognise your pain... you had the fortitude to make justice happen. You provided a role model for many women in similar circumstances and gave them hope."

I hadn't seen Linda in a couple of decades, but we'd reconnected online. I can't say that I really know her as an adult, beyond what anyone puts on social media. But her experience of being a by-stander to my speaking out about rape was largely one of hope. She believed that I'd created change through my strength and sheer force of will; that I could be encouraging important conversations held by rape victims themselves: that if they're up for the fight, then anything's possible.

As I mulled over these responses and many more, I asked Gavin what he thought of being along for the last few years. I'd only met him after I went public with my rape, and we'd originally met in a work context. We didn't start out talking about my story – we started out talking about data and research and how it can make communications campaigns easier and more effective. It felt like perhaps his point of view would matter the most: had my story had an impact on someone outside of the usual conversations about rape, who hadn't known me before?

"I've learned a huge amount from you," he said. "But it's impossible to enumerate everything I've learned. I am now far more likely to talk about sexual violence and the justice system and be more outraged than I would ever have been before. I do feel informed and empowered in some ways."

For Kat, Linda and Gavin, as well as many more who I won't quote here, I'd made my story clearer by explaining the context and by speaking about the data that underlined everything. By doing that, I've made it easier for them to talk about not just any individual story, but the wider issues at play.

I'd become a bit of an expert, and in sharing what I'd learned, had helped drive the conversations they were having. For me, these conversations are key. If we can finally acknowledge that rape makes us uncomfortable, or perhaps even just accept that it's entirely human nature to want to believe someone when they say they haven't committed rape, or to believe that there is something about a victim that contributes to their rape, then we can begin to re-humanise rape victims themselves. Perhaps we can make a difference across each individual conversation, and victims will start to feel believed, police officers will grow in their understanding of how to investigate rape and the CPS will present rape cases to juries who are not weighed down by a whole range of rape myths.

Chapter Ten

In late September 2015, just over six months after the assault, I was sitting on a London bus on my way to work on a fresh autumn morning. Since I'd woken up in that hotel bed next to John, and since that first hyperventilating panic attack at the hotel, everything had changed for me.

My daughter and I were adjusting to being more or less a team of two. I'd just started a new job – exactly the sort of job I'd been hoping to find. While I was having a difficult time – and would still occasionally find myself in a panic, unable to catch my breath, or struggling to concentrate, or being easily irritated or upset – it did feel at that point like things could be going in the right direction.

The police had warned me not to seek any therapy or professional support, as they saw it as endangering the case if it went to court. They'd told me that the defence could obtain notes from any sessions with a therapist which would make taking a case forward more difficult. So, without help, I was coping as best I could and I thought I was doing okay. Not perfect, but okay. And life was carrying on in a way where I felt that I could trust that things were going to get better.

But that moment – just as I was feeling like things could improve for me and that life was moving in the right direction, blissfully unaware and sitting on a light-filled London bus on my way to work – was the last time I fully believed in our country's criminal justice system.

Before that moment, I'd assumed that seeking justice would be personally difficult, horribly invasive and deeply overwhelming, but that the path from reporting a rape, through a police investigation, to the prosecutors charging my attacker and the case going to court, would be straightforward. I assumed that to be the reality both for me, but also for anyone else who'd been raped and who'd then involved the police.

That moment was the last time I trusted that the system could work.

At 9:13am, that sun-filled autumn moment was broken by the alert of an email from the police as it popped into my phone's inbox. Attached was a letter dated 10 days earlier from the CPS.

"Dear Miss Hunt," it began. "Thank you for telling the police about what happened to you. I appreciate how difficult it can be to report allegations such as these."

I skimmed down the page until I found the only part that mattered, buried in the third paragraph.

"As the specialist rape prosecutor responsible for your case I have been working closely with Detective Constable Caroline Smithson[118] to see whether there is enough evidence to bring a prosecution. After carefully considering all the available information and discussing it with DC Smithson, I have decided there is not enough evidence for any charges to be brought."

They would not be taking my case forward. I was not a worthy enough victim. There would be no justice.

---

118   Some names have been changed.

The world tunnelled into darkness in front of me, my breath caught in my chest and I almost fainted. I tried to keep reading, trying to understand how this could have happened and what it all meant.

"As the prosecutor in your case," it continued, "I have to follow the tests set out in the Code for Crown Prosecutors. This means I can only charge a suspect with a criminal offence if I am satisfied that a jury hearing the case is more likely than not to find the defendant guilty. Otherwise, a prosecution cannot go ahead, no matter how serious it is. The officer can supply you with a leaflet which gives more information about my role.

"I have carefully considered all the evidence provided by the police and have come to the conclusion that there are too many weaknesses in the evidence collected, which means the high threshold of proof needed for a criminal prosecution is simply not there."

For days afterwards, I read and re-read and read again the letter. Over and over and over. I simply could not imagine a world where our criminal justice system wouldn't take a case like mine seriously and where my attacker would avoid having to face a jury. It felt like the world was upside down from the one I thought I knew.

But that letter, that moment of finding out that my attacker would never answer for his crime, is the exact sort of news that almost all rape victims currently receive in this country. As discussed earlier, as of January of 2022, 98.7% of victims who report their rape to the police receive some version of my letter: we will not be prosecuting. We are not seeking justice. Your attacker will never have to answer for this horrible crime. And that letter will almost always feel like it says, "You are not worthy."

And that's not okay. Because we are worthy.

In my case, it took years for me to unpick the evidence and determine just how flawed both the police and CPS were in investigating John and in their decision-making around my case. Indeed, in that letter from September and the follow-up in October 2015, no mention was made of the crimes they were considering charging John with. Even worse, to this day, the police and CPS insist they did nothing wrong. The CPS even repeatedly refused to offer me an apology for forcing me to bring a judicial review in the voyeurism case, even in light of the Richards case.[119] They continue to act as though the vast majority of rape victims aren't worthy of justice, full stop.

While we were bringing my judicial review against the CPS to clarify the law on voyeurism, Kate Ellis and the Centre for Women's Justice team were also bringing another judicial review against the CPS on behalf of the End Violence Against Women Coalition (EVAW), to determine whether or not prosecutors had acted unlawfully in unofficially changing their guidance on when a rape case should be taken forward.

The prosecutor on my case told me that the CPS had to believe that a jury would be more likely than not to convict, and that they were bound to the Full Test Code, meaning a case has to be

---

119   Throughout the complaints process, the CPS refused my complaint and denied that I deserved an apology. In October 2021, however, the Independent Assessor of Complaints for the CPS upheld my complaint and directed them to apologise to me. The apology I received only covered issues around poor communications and timeliness and not the many other things the IAC upheld my complaint on.

51% winnable to go forward.[120] But, as discussed in Chapter Three, the CPS began instructing its prosecutors in 2016 to only take rape cases forward if they felt that the case had a greater than 60% chance of a jury convicting.[121]

From 2016 until 2021, England and Wales saw the charging rate in rape cases fall relentlessly, year after year, with prosecutions falling by 70%.[122] Regardless of that irrefutable fact, in and out of court, the CPS denied there had been a change in the way they prosecuted rape. Even though they acknowledged the new 60% benchmark,[123] they denied it had changed anything, while being unable to provide any alternative reason for the decline in cases being brought forward. In the end, the court was bound to take the CPS's word for it and as a result, was unable to take into account the evidence

---

120   See Chapter Three.

121   First reported in the *Guardian* in 2018 (https://www.theguardian.com/law/2018/sep/24/prosecutors-rape-cases-cps-crown-prosecution-service-conviction-rates) before being the subject of a judicial review which uncovered the specifics of this so-called "touch of the tiller" instruction.

122   https://www.theguardian.com/law/2021/jul/22/cps-accused-of-betraying-victims-as-prosecutions-hit-record-low

123   https://www.bbc.co.uk/news/uk-56402068

amassed[124] by the Centre for Women's Justice and EVAW that showed otherwise.

In response to this finding, the CPS released a statement amounting to not much less than a victory lap. They clearly felt vindicated, even though there had been enough of a case for the courts to have allowed the judicial review to go forward in a two-day hearing in the first place.[125] It shouldn't have been about winning on a technicality, it should have been a learning experience, a growing moment. It wasn't. Worse, the Director of Public Prosecutions, Max Hill QC, was quoted in the statement as saying, "I share the deep public concern that, while the number of rape allegations has increased significantly in recent years, the number going to court has fallen. The CPS is actively involved in the cross-government review which has been working for almost two years to understand and address the reasons behind the trend. While that work continues, it is clear no single factor has led to the

---

124   https://www.centreforwomensjustice.org.uk/news/ 2020/6/29/lpti6p5e19unqglo7wd9mm68d621b7
125   There is a very high bar to reach for the courts to allow a judicial review to go forward to a hearing.

drop in cases, and meaningful change will need a system-wide approach."[126]

When the CPS says that change is needed in a system-wide approach, those in the know will tell you that means it's everyone else's fault. That the police need to do better. That the courts need to do better. That everyone needs to do better and take action to right the ship.

Everyone except the CPS.

In the face of the huge amount of evidence about the failure of the CPS to prosecute rape cases, and the undeniable nationwide plunge in the number of rape cases going to court (even though the number of cases reported to the police has increased), the CPS continues to deny it has done anything wrong, or even has any accountability for the situation.[127]

The CPS has seemingly failed to understand that there is a problem, and that we victims deserve a criminal justice system that understands that rape

---

126   https://www.cps.gov.uk/cps/news/cps-statement-judg-ment-judicial-review-prosecution-rape-and-serious-sexual-offences
127   For example, see this set of interviews given to *Channel 4 News* by rape and serious sexual offences prosecutors: https://www.youtube.com/watch?v=w-U-PWtkpsU

is not acceptable, that women very infrequently lie about rape, and that unprosecuted rapists go on to rape again.

They don't seem to care about us. But, worse, right now we have no other options.

The Crown Prosecution Service is constitutionally independent[128] from the police, from the government, from the judiciary, from anyone. It was established in this way in the 1980s to help tackle what was seen as a corrupt policing system, and there are absolutely good arguments for not allowing politicians to determine who is prosecuted and who isn't in individual cases. However, what this means in practice is that while the CPS is superintended by the Attorney General and subject to inspections from Her Majesty's Crown Prosecution Service Inspectorate (HMCPSI), there is very little anyone inside or outside of the government can do to reward them for doing well, or impose consequences for failure to do their jobs effectively.

---

128   Unlike in the United States, as the UK has no written constitution, just saying that something is "constitutional" doesn't actually make it any more difficult to change legislatively than anything else. It's more a statement of principle than of law.

Chapter Ten

In 2018, HMCPSI published a report recommending that the CPS needed to urgently fix the way they communicate with victims through letters. They might as well have used the same report two years later when they revisited the issue. The CPS had not improved in any real way. They had no drive to do so, and, as it made no difference whether they responded or not, they could simply ignore the issue.

After John's sentencing, Kate filed a detailed complaint with the CPS over how they'd treated me. I was mainly asking for an apology – particularly for having been forced to bring a judicial review on the voyeurism case when they were arguing two sides of the same law in two different cases. I was also asking for them to learn from their mistakes. I fully expected that in response to my complaint I wouldn't receive an actual apology, but something along the lines of "We're sorry you feel that way," or "We're sorry that was difficult for you," and that would be that. I genuinely couldn't imagine that, given everything the CPS had put me through and that had been commented on in the press and in legal circles for years, they would say I didn't deserve an apology and continue to insist they'd done nothing wrong, even when they'd lied to me[129] or made legal errors. But that's exactly what happened: they refused to apologise. I ended up having to appeal this decision all the way through the CPS complaints system to the Independent Assessor of Complaints (IAC). In October 2021, the IAC upheld my complaint and recommended that the CPS apologise to me. That was in its small way gratifying, but when I asked what this meant in practice, what consequences there would be for the CPS, I was told that my complaint being upheld was the outcome: there was nothing more. The CPS was not obliged to do anything with the findings.

The CPS is funded entirely by the taxpayer but is not in any way accountable to us. In most cases, we hold public bodies to account through ministers, who are themselves answerable to the Prime Minister who appoints them, and to the public through the ballot box. But the head of the CPS is not a political appointment; they cannot be fired by the Prime Minister or even by a new government when it takes over. Indeed, as far as I can tell, the

---

129 For example, when they told me in 2016 that John had not masturbated onto me, as discussed in Chapter One.

head of the CPS can't be fired by the person who appointed them.[130] From the moment they walk in the door, they are seemingly untouchable for the five years of their term.

And this lack of accountability is, frankly, an experiment that has failed. It's time for us to consider what can and should be done, urgently, to address this. Real change to the way we prosecute rape in this country is likely going to need real change to the criminal justice system.[131]

But even beyond structural change to the criminal justice system, there's more we can do. There's more that we need to do. And we need to do it now. Prosecuting rape cases successfully requires real change across all areas of society. As much as we need to recognise that the police are human and take their very human understanding of rape

---

130   As a civil servant, the Director of Public Prosecutions can technically be fired by the Cabinet Secretary.

131   As noted earlier, the CPS is failing to prosecute crime in general. So, while the need for criminal justice reform is seen most acutely with rape and other serious sexual offence cases, they're frankly just a canary in the coal mine. It's not that the CPS is bad at prosecuting rape and good at everything else. They are fundamentally bad at doing their job: prosecuting criminals and protecting the public from further harm.

to work, so too do prosecutors. And judges. But crucially, so too do juries.

In studies of how rape victims feel about disclosing what happened to them, reasons for not telling people include shame and guilt, not wanting certain people to find out about it and a fear of not being believed.[132] Rape victims have been dehumanised by their attacker, their control has been taken away and they are often aware enough of rape myths and victim-blaming to be afraid of not being taken seriously. If they report the rape to the police, many interactions with the criminal justice system will be tinged with these same issues, further compounded by those around them believing rape to be something that happens to people they don't know, that a victim can and should prevent their own rape or that the victim did something to cause the rape.

In their pursuit of justice, if their case is one of the 1.3% that actually sees a court, a victim faces a disbelieving police force, an obstructive prosecutor, a judiciary with old-fashioned ideas and a jury made of

132 http://www.middlebury.edu/media/view/240971/original/sable_article.pdf

normal, everyday people – who believe rape myths just as much as other normal, everyday people. But, as discussed in Chapter Three, research has shown that if the judge educates the jury on the fallacy of rape myths, they're more likely to convict.[133] Juries aren't made up of robots, they're people from our society and their beliefs can change. If juries' innate bias against and disbelief in rape victims can be counteracted, this should clearly be implemented across our society.

Not just with juries, but with the people around us.

When a rape victim chooses to talk about what happened to them, we must *listen*.

We must, in our conversations, encourage others to listen. We have to put aside our own gut instinct and remember: 97–98% of the time, if someone says they've been raped, they've been raped. We have to remind others of this fact every time it comes up in conversation. We have to remember that rape victims almost always suffer traumatic stress responses in the two weeks after the assault, and that 50% suffer from PTSD for months afterwards, meaning their reactions to stress can be totally out

---

133   Leverick, F. (2020) "What do we know about rape myths and juror decision making?" *International Journal of Evidence and Proof.*

of step with what we imagine as normal. We have to remind those around us that this is true. And then we have to remind ourselves that rapists have no favourite type of target; rape victims have nothing in common other than often being female and between 16 and 65. Therefore a rape victim doesn't do anything to make them the sort of person that gets raped.[134] We must have this uncomfortable conversation with those around us when sexual violence comes up. Because otherwise, we have no hope.

It is in our own understanding and in our conversations with others that we can begin to breakdown the stereotypes, stigmas and myths that surround rape – and we can choose to believe victims and remind those around us that, statistically speaking, it's *almost never* wrong to believe someone who says they've been raped.

And these conversations have to start. Urgently. It's only in talking about rape that we have any chance of tackling it. Talking about it will help on

---

134   Put slightly more crassly, a woman should be able to walk down the street drunk and naked and have us not blame her for being raped. Choosing to be naked or drunk is not the same as consenting to sex, though obviously, walking down the street naked would be ill-advised if only for legal reasons.

three fronts: preventing rape, supporting victims of rape and finally improving the chances of the prosecution of rape.

Currently, our police and prosecutors believe that a rape case isn't worth pursuing 98.7% of the time, the reason often being (as with Kat's case) that they don't believe a jury can understand rape.

But they're wrong.

We know better and can do better. Cases need to be put in front of juries and we'll do the rest; every conversation we have about the reality of sexual violence could help someone realise that straying across that grey line is not okay.

And we are going to have those conversations.

We need to talk about rape, because otherwise it remains acceptable both to commit it and to fail to prosecute it.

The day before John's sentencing hearing, I was invited to have coffee at 10 Downing Street with a member of the political staff. It was informal and arranged through an acquaintance. Over the summer, I'd read that the Prime Minister was considering imposing a sort of quota system on the CPS to force them to prosecute more rapes. The newspapers wrote that the Prime Minister and the Cabinet were mortified by the continued fall in rape prosecution rates and the deafening lack of accountability and transparency from the CPS in response to victim complaint after victim complaint. The lack of rape prosecutions wasn't just an embarrassment from the government's point of view, but a disaster. I wanted to help fix it.

As I sat in the waiting area just beyond the big black door, with security and the portrait of Sir Robert Walpole, I quickly scribbled out my wish list for the meeting in a notebook balanced on my knee. I wrote down that we needed the number of rape prosecutions to go up. I wrote down that we needed to recognise that rapists are often serial offenders. I wrote down that I wanted to find a way to encourage early guilty pleas. I wrote down that we needed to find a way to dispel rape myths and, even more so, work to counteract them with the police, CPS and judiciary. And finally, I wrote down that victims needed to be provided with better support, however and whenever they needed it.

I didn't want to talk about my story or add my voice to the raft of complaints about how the CPS treats individual rape victims. I wanted to talk about real change in the system. And we did. That and more. In the end, I was invited back – three times in 10 days. I kept meeting more and more people who were just as concerned as I was about the way that rape victims were falling through the cracks and rapists were escaping justice. When I was offered a job as an expert advisor for the government two months later, it dawned on me that everything I'd learned in the previous few years could really be put to good use.

From victim, to law changer, to expert advisor for the government.

The path seemed impossible, but there I was. On it.

Epilogue

In September 2021, I sat at my dining table, with the blind pulled up on my front windows. My laptop was open and staring unblinkingly at me. I was about to give a virtual talk on my experience of being a rape victim trying to find justice to the College of Policing as part of a training day for police forces across the country. The title of my talk was: "Why me? A victim's experience of the criminal justice system."

As part of her opening speech, Sarah Crew, the national lead for policing on adult rape and interim Chief Constable for Avon & Somerset, spoke about some of the work we'd done together since I'd joined the government as an expert advisor. I could see myself blushing slightly in the video conference camera, as she spoke about how I'd worked to bring the voice of a victim to the centre of the government's conversations on how to do better on prosecuting rape.

Most poignantly, however, Sarah reminded the attendees that the victims they deal with as part of their investigations are exactly that: victims. That while police officers may be working across a number of sex offence cases, each individual matters as a victim. And that while police officers may forget a victim or their story when the case has been closed, the victim will never forget the police officer, especially the one who treated them badly.

The night before my talk, I had thrown out my carefully written speech. It was too angry, too detailed and too unhelpful. For the better part of a year, I'd been advising ministers and officials as part of the government's End-to-End Rape Review, trying both to unpick what had gone so terribly wrong that almost no rape victims in this country ever saw justice and also, crucially, how to change it.

There are many reasons why the criminal justice system has been failing victims – many of which I've talked about earlier in this book. The main thing I discovered in my government role was the extent to which our country's police forces and prosecutors approach rape cases differently to other crimes. By and large they do not start off by investigating what happened or looking into the suspect's background. Instead, they look at the victim to determine whether or not she or he is "credible".

Before beginning my work on the Rape Review, I knew that victims often spoke about feeling as though they were the ones being investigated. I had felt exactly like that. And the reality is, those feelings are justified.

Until now, it has been absolutely true that the victims have been the ones in the spotlight first and foremost. It hasn't even been standard practice to check a rape suspect's name to see if they've previously been in trouble for something similar, until the victim has jumped that nearly impossible hurdle of being deemed credible. Very few victims see justice, because, along the way, some part of the criminal justice system decides they are not believable or worthy. The case is dropped and the victim sees no justice.

And that's a big deal for the two reasons I wrote about in the early chapters of this book.

Firstly, the reality is that the vast majority of people who report a rape are telling the truth.

The second reason makes our country's abysmal rape prosecution rate all the more horrifying: rapists are very often serial offenders.

Academic research has been showing this for decades. There is a greater than 50/50 chance an unprosecuted rapist will rape again. More importantly, research from early 2021 with Sarah Crew's force in Avon & Somerset found that nearly a quarter of the time, those named in a sex offence case had already been named in connection with at least one earlier sex offence. Fully 60% of them were known to the police for one reason or another. This essentially further validates the premise that rapists rape, not that victims somehow get themselves raped.

The research in Avon & Somerset led the force to change the way it investigates rape; it now looks into the background of the suspect at the beginning of an investigation rather than the end – if at all. And indeed, the findings from the force's Project Bluestone were so striking that the Home Secretary then wrote to all Chief Constables to ask them to do the same.

I was standing up, albeit virtually, in front of more than 100 police officers to talk about this fantastic and fundamental shift in the way they were going to start investigating rape: by starting with the rapist.

"Last night, I threw out my talk and started over," I began, "and it's a good thing I did. Because I absolutely have to take a moment to reflect on what Sarah just said. She reminded you that a victim meets you on the worst day of their life. That while it's your job, and a day at the office for you to confront sexual violence – no victim signed up for this. They don't want to talk with you, they don't want to need the police.

"I remember, distinctly, the two police officers who came to my house the morning after I was raped. I remember the light behind them through the window. The way they sat in my dining table chairs. The way one grabbed my phone out of my hand to go through it. The way they looked at me, disbelieving and uncaring.

"I will always remember their names. Don't be the officer who a rape victim remembers for all of the wrong reasons."

I then went on to talk about four things: why I was raped, including some of the details of the case; why I was failed by the police; why I was failed by the CPS; and why I was trying to bring a victim's voice into government.

I told them I was raped because someone thought they could get away with it. Because they thought there was nothing wrong with having sex with someone who could barely stand, who they thought might be on drugs or mentally ill.

I said that it was mostly just because I was there.

As I told my story, questions and comments started to pop up in the chat bar on the right; I mostly ignored them: I was telling my story and knew there'd be time for questions at the end.

And then I saw the first of what would be a few questions from one particular officer: "At some point you and your father parted company that evening, what happened immediately after is what I am wondering? Left a drink unattended, shared a drink or accepted one from a stranger?"

It was not an innocent question.

Instead, I expect it was the tip of the iceberg for this particular officer. His starting point in hearing my account was to think, "but surely, she must have done something to encourage this."

This was the exact problem at the heart of rape prosecution – he began by looking at me and my story. He began by questioning what I'd done to cause my rape. He began by passing judgement on the worth of my case and my worthiness as a victim. Within moments of hearing my story, he wasn't asking questions about the suspect's behaviour or past or motivation, he was instead sitting as judge and jury and already deciding this wasn't a case worth taking forward, this wasn't a worthy victim.

This is exactly why it's so crucial for the police and the CPS to commit to a suspect-focused investigation model,[135] rather than it being yet another great policy written down but then ignored.

Rapists rape, and they're the ones that need investigating, not their victims.

---

135   The Joint National Action Plan on RASSO 2021 spells out that both the police and the CPS will train their staff on suspect-focused investigation. The training I was a part of was one of many options offered to police officers to fulfil that. I've not had the opportunity to see any of the CPS training and so can't comment on it. Details on the JNAP: https://www.cps.gov.uk/sites/default/files/documents/publications/RASSO-JNAP-2021-v1-0.pdf

Epilogue

*　*　*

One of the contributions I made to the Rape Review that I am most proud of was an understanding that we can and must do better for victims. That rape suspects need to be investigated up front, rather than decisions being made about whether cases should go forward or not based on how likeable or credible a victim seems. That victims need to be supported through the criminal justice system because every person who reports a crime is doing so not just for themselves, but for all of us.

On the day that the Review was launched, I sent an email to my supporters about how everything on the original list that I wrote – in a notebook balanced on my knee, sitting on a sofa, waiting to meet someone at Number 10 for the first time – was in the Review. There was a lot for us all to celebrate.

But, perhaps, there are two more things to be proud of. The first is that things have already started to change. When that police officer made clear through his questions that he thought that a woman who drinks in public, or accepts a drink from someone, is in effect causing their own rape – and then went on to make comments about false rape allegations being a hugely prevalent issue – other officers stepped in. They made it clear that this thinking was unacceptable and outdated. One of the attendees messaged me later to say that they had reported the situation to the officer's boss, and at least 10 people watching the talk reached out to apologise that the situation had happened at all. And this is just part of the change that's happening.

And then the strangest thing happened: this policy shift to a suspect-focused investigation model had a very personal impact on me.

On a dark Friday afternoon in November, about two months after that College of Policing talk, I was finishing up some work after a long week. Usually on a Friday afternoon, I'd have been racing out the door to collect my daughter from her school bus, but she wasn't coming home that night. I wasn't needed for anything until the following day and I had a night to myself. I was working across two computers perched on the end of my dining table, wrapping up leftover tasks from the week and relishing the quiet and unexpected time to leisurely finish everything up. And then my phone rang out of the blue and my story took a very strange and unexpected turn.

In the course of investigating a different crime, the police had read and really considered a tweet that John had posted the summer before.[136]

"I don't know if you remember this," started Detective Constable Charlie Bakesy, "but last summer, there was this tweet where he..."

"The one that seemed like a rape confession?" I interrupted.

"Yes," he said, "that one. Here's the thing, I was looking at it again, and it really does seem to be a confession. He's written about you waking up after he had sex with you."

"Which is rape," I said matter-of-factly, still entirely unsure of where the conversation was going. A sleeping person, obviously, cannot consent to sex.

"So, I'm calling to let you know that we're viewing that tweet as new evidence in the rape case, which we've now reopened. The original crime reference number has been reactivated on our computer system."

"Wait," I paused for a moment trying to understand what he was saying. "Wait, what?"

On a dark November afternoon in 2021, DC

---

136   See Chapter 1, footnote 5 – a footnote that I wrote months before this phone call.

Bakesy[137] was ringing to let me know that on the basis of a tweet, that six and a half years after my rape, the police were reopening the rape case. To DC Bakesy's mind, the tweet read like a confession of rape – it had looked like that to me, too, when I first saw it, so much so that I considered filing a new police report on my rape and citing that tweet. But after all of my experiences with the police before, I had decided not to bother, because nothing was ever going to change. I was never going to see any justice and it was foolish to hope otherwise.

But suddenly everything was different. DC Bakesy went on to explain that he'd spoken with his colleagues and with the CPS and that he was going to put together a case file with the tweet as new evidence and submit it to the prosecutors for a fresh decision on whether or not to charge John with rape.

Suddenly there was this glimmer, almost like a mirage on the horizon, shimmering and shaking in the distance. It was this deeply unlikely possibility that there could actually be justice in my rape case, a little shred of hope appearing in this most unlikely of places, at the least expected time. Before I'd even

---

137   Names have been changed for privacy.

hung up the phone, I had begun to daydream about what it could be like to see John face a jury for his crime. It was almost too much to contemplate.

I often say that all victims of rape have a story all their own at the beginning. Their experience is unique. But by the end, almost all of our stories end the same way. That shimmering mirage gave me a moment of wonder: could my story, more than six and a half years later, have a different ending to the 98.7% of rape victims whose cases end in no charges being brought?

I had never expected any of my work to actually impact me, or my case. But every conversation I had over the next six weeks with DC Bakesy about the case was mind-blowing in how different the police were approaching the case this time. Originally, DC Bakesy expected his part to be quick: he was going to write up the evidence from the tweet and resubmit the original file to the CPS for a decision. That was before he'd seen the original file.

I'd known from conversations with Kate, but also with Matthew Smith and the QC he brought on to the case, that the police had written very unprofessional and inappropriate things about me in their notes. I knew that they had decided from early on that I was unworthy of their efforts and that the investigation was flawed from the start. I also expected that the file they submitted to the CPS in the first place in 2015 was likely to conclude that I was not the 'right sort of victim' for them. I warned DC Bakesy that he might want to allow for a bit more time than he was expecting – that I suspected that the original file probably needed to be reworked with more of a suspect focus. I don't think he fully understood until he dug into the file.

It took until the end of December for DC Bakesy to go back through the evidence, re-question John and submit the file to the CPS for a decision. As he read through the previous file, he was shocked by how stacked everything was against me.

When he looked at the CCTV footage of John and I going from Poison to the hotel, he saw a deeply intoxicated person, who didn't have full use of their arms and was clearly, visibly, profoundly affected by drink or drugs. When he compared what he saw to what was written in the file – that the CCTV didn't show anything – it became clear to him that he was going to have to start over. Indeed, when the file was submitted to the CPS, the CCTV was regarded as new evidence alongside the tweet. It showed that clearly, a reasonable person would not have thought that I was in any fit state to consent to anything.

Previously, the police had looked for every reason to discredit me, and didn't look at John. This time was different. Just before the new year, the file was submitted to the prosecutors for a fresh decision and the waiting began. The police were hopeful. They thought it was a really strong case, especially given everything that they now knew about him and his behaviour.

But the hope was a mirage... Of course, the CPS declined to prosecute. In declining to take the case, they wrote to me that there were multiple defences that John could use in court. Instead of writing about the evidence, instead of writing about John saying that he thought I might be on drugs or a bit mad, instead of writing about the CCTV evidence of my being obviously impaired, they wrote that there was no "scientific evidence" to my being too intoxicated to consent to sex. Their excuse was that they didn't believe that a jury could be trusted with the case. But their letter didn't seem to be applying the Full Test

Code – that a case must be 51% winnable in front of a jury – they seemed to be expecting a case to be 100% winnable before taking it forward.

The police considered filing an appeal themselves, but DC Bakesy's boss rang me to explain that they were aware that the CPS would have ratified the decision to not prosecute at a level quite high up in the organisation – and that there wasn't really a point in fighting it. The police thought it was strong, thought that the prosecutors should take it forward, but the CPS wasn't willing to prosecute John.

While the police had changed immeasurably in their approach to the case – the CPS continued to judge me as a victim, and concluded I was not worthy. There will never be justice for me. But I never thought there would be, and that's not why I started working with the government. I started because I wanted to make sure that tomorrow's victims are treated better than I was, that they are seen as worthy of justice regardless of who they are. I started to do this work because I wanted to see more rapists face a court. We're not there yet. There is so much more to do.

Epilogue

But things are moving in the right direction. In my life, I see more people starting to recognise there's something very wrong with the way we speak about, and think about, sexual violence. As a society, we are starting to move in the right direction, but we need more. Every time someone starts to blame a victim for their rape, we need someone else to speak up. We cannot be silent any more on this, we cannot let the conversation pass.

We need to talk.

The most important thing to come out of this journey, for me, though, isn't any of that. The most important thing for me is that my daughter has learned from watching me through the years that if there's something about the world that you think is wrong, then you can and should go change it. She is young and doesn't yet know any of the details of what happened to me, but she has watched as I climbed out of the hole I'd been in, held down by despair. She watched me as I tried to find a meaning in what happened to me and started to fight to make sure that other victims wouldn't face what I faced.

On the day that the Criminal Appeals Court ruled in our favour, clarifying the law on voyeurism, my daughter proudly declared that now Hunt girls change the law on Tuesdays. As though it were a very normal thing. Because for her, she thinks it is.

As a single mother, my childcare inevitably seemed to let me down whenever I had to attend a meeting, so my daughter has been by my side through much of this journey. When she was seven, she ended up addressing constituency letters and photocopying with a research assistant while I met with an MP. Just after her 11th birthday, she introduced herself to Cabinet Office officials as my intern, with a laugh. She's been to Number 10 with me, she's been to the Ministry of Justice. She sat by my side in the gallery above the House of Commons as my MP pleaded my case on changing the law on voyeurism.

She is why I'm here, and how I got through the darkest times. I hope that what I've done has made this country a bit better for her when she's older. But most of all, I hope that she now will have the power to go out and make the country what she wants and needs it to be. It'll be hers soon, after all. And she'll have her own conversations to start.

Acknowledgements

This book could not have existed without the encouragement of Gavin Devine, who reassured me constantly throughout writing it that it was worthwhile and important. But I also couldn't have gotten through the last few years of living this story without his friendship and support. I am incredibly lucky to have him in my life. Thank you so much, Gavin.

The story itself would have been entirely different – and without justice – had it not been for Kate Ellis, Harriet Wistrich and everyone at the Centre for Women's Justice. Thank you for your work on my cases. Your support has been invaluable.

Thank you to my agent, Alice Saunders at the Soho Agency, and my editor, Jo Sollis at Mardle

Books, for believing in this book and its importance. Many thanks as well to Nick Simmonds and Patricia Seabright for their amazing support as we all worked on our books, together but apart, over lockdown. My colleagues Lucy Parker and Tarini Kumar provided much appreciated fresh eyes, feedback and advice on the full draft, and helped me see that it really was worth publishing – thank you both.

With huge appreciation and love for my family: Shelley Hunt, Margaret Abelkop and Gabriel Hudson. Not only have they been supportive and wonderful and kept me going over the last many years, but they literally helped make sure I could work on this book while on holiday, in Hershey Park, next to the lazy river – and I am so happy to have them and the many adventures we have had, and will have, together.

I also have had support from my amazing friends including Victor, Jannon, Kitty, Rushnara, Mandy, Olivia, Kat, Emily, Nimco, Josh, Cleo and Catherine. Every glass of champagne in person or over Zoom, every supper together, every bit of childcare, every hang out, and every shoulder to cry on over the last few very difficult years has been so appreciated. Thank you for carrying me forward when I thought I couldn't keep fighting.

There are far too many people to name who have helped me get to where I am now. From journalists to MPs to Special Advisors to people on social media spreading my story to those who helped me crowdfund to those who reached out to make sure I was okay every time there was a difficult story in the news. Thank you for all of it.

And finally, thank you to every amazing teacher I ever had, who helped me become the person I am, but especially thank you to Linda Kruegel, my high school chemistry teacher. Who could see me as me, even though I was terrible at chemistry.

Dear reader,

I have what may seem like an odd request.

Now that you've read this book, you know that I think that we all need to talk about sexual violence. That I want to start conversations about why we don't talk about rape; that the only cause of rape is rapists; who commits rape and why; why society defaults to blaming the victim; and ultimately how we need to change and humanise the way we talk about rape in order to truly hear and support victims and end the current epidemic of sexual violence.

We need to bring these conversations out of the shadows and let victims know we are on their side. And we all need to challenge our prejudices and preconceived ideas. Above all, we need to talk and we need to demand change.

I wrote this book very much as a way to start those conversations, but I know full well that not everyone is going to buy this book. But I want as many people to read it as possible.

You'll see that on the next page is a place to write the date that you finished the book, but there are 10 slots.

So I have a favour to ask: now that you've finished reading it, instead of keeping this book on your shelf, would you consider sharing it? And, more so, ask the person you give it to to also do the same? If you are happy to do so — please share on your social media, too.

If this copy reaches ten people we will together have done so much to stimulate a better conversation.

Because, of course, We Need To Talk.

Thank you,
Emily

#weneedtotalk
#ProsecuteRape
#LifeAftetRape

Would you consider sharing this book?

Write you first name and
the date and then pass it on.

1. _____

2. _____

3. _____

4. _____

5. _____

6. _____

7. _____

8. _____

9. _____

10. _____

Phone: 0808 500 2222

The 24/7 Rape and Sexual Abuse Support Line is a confidential emotional support and listening service for anyone aged 16 or over in England and Wales who has experienced sexual violence or abuse at some point in their life. It is totally free and open 24 hours a day, 365 days a year by phone and webchat.

The specially trained advisers answering calls understand how complex and varied different experiences of sexual violence and abuse can be. They will help victims and survivors better understand what has happened to them and talk through what their next steps might be – including help to find longer-term support.

Anybody who calls this line will be listened to, believed, and will never be judged.

How to help a friend who's been raped

If you've been approached by a friend for help after rape, you may feel worried about how best to support them. There's no 'right' reaction to rape, so it's important that you don't make assumptions about how your friend should behave or feel.

The first thing that you should say to your friend is that you believe them and are here to support them in any way that you can. Remember, you might be the first person they have told.

Things to remember:
- be patient
- stay calm and don't worry about silences
- let them talk

Here are some key things to consider if a friend has confided in you:

1. If they blame themselves, reassure them. It's important that you challenge any self-blame and continue to reassure your friend that it isn't their

fault. Seek advice and support for your friend so they feel able to challenge any 'victim-blaming'.

2. Understand that they may feel confused or unsure. It is not unusual if they're uncertain about what has happened or if they struggle to remember. It's important for you to acknowledge your friend's feelings and take on board what they are saying.

3. Check your own emotions. Withholding your emotions is important. You may feel angry about what's happened, but it's important that you don't let that dominate the conversation.

4. Don't push for details. If they're not ready to talk about it, be patient.

5. Never report the rape to the police or anyone else without their consent if they are an adult. They need to be in control of the situation. You can talk to them about reporting to the police, but it is their decision to make.

6. Remind them to carry out health checks. It may not be something they want to talk about, but it's important that they undertake health checks, such as for STIs, as well as a pregnancy test. You can put them in touch with their local Sexual

Assault Referral Centre (SARC) which provides services to victims and survivors of rape or sexual assault whether or not they choose to report the offence to the police.

7. Keep in touch. Call them, text them and let them know that you're around if they need you.

8. Get support. If you want to seek help to support your friend, contact an Independent Sexual Violence Advisor service (ISVA) or Victim Support's free, 24/7 Supportline on 08 08 16 89 111.

If your friend is under the age of 16, the rape should be reported to the police and to children's safeguarding.

Find out more about how we can help after rape or sexual assault via the Victim Support website: victimsupport.org.uk.